Isaac B Rich

Gazelle

A True Tale of the Great Rebellion and other Poems

Isaac B Rich

Gazelle

A True Tale of the Great Rebellion and other Poems

ISBN/EAN: 9783337145910

Printed in Europe, USA, Canada, Australia, Japan

Cover: Foto ©Thomas Meinert / pixelio.de

More available books at **www.hansebooks.com**

GAZELLE,

A True Tale

OF

THE GREAT REBELLION;

AND

OTHER POEMS.

BOSTON:
LEE & SHEPARD,
149 WASHINGTON STREET.
NEW YORK: THE AMERICAN NEWS CO.,
121 NASSAU STREET.
1866.

Entered, according to Act of Congress, in the year 1865, by
ISAAC B. RICH,
In the Clerk's Office of the District Court of the District of Massachusetts.

STEREOTYPED BY C. J. PETERS & SON,
No. 13, Washington Street.

CONTENTS.

	PAGE
DEDICATION	5
GAZELLE: A TALE OF THE GREAT REBELLION	9
WORSHIP	175
"WE WRITE BLESSINGS IN SAND, EVILS IN MARBLE"	177
THE HERO'S BURIAL	180
LITTLE ZOE; MY WIFE	183
CHANGELESS	185
THE DRAGOON'S RETREAT	186
THE FRIEND I HAD	188
SADNESS	190
HALLY	191
ANNA SHADER	193
GOOD-BY	194

DEDICATED

TO

The Angel I saw in my Dream.

———oo:o:oo———

I HAD such an exquisite dream last night,
　As I lay on my couch asleep,
That though it is June, and the earth is bright,
　I only awoke to weep.
I dreamed that a flower which last winter froze
　'Neath the storms from the pelting skies,
And folded its petals under the snows,
　Away from our loving eyes,
Revived, in the light of its loveliness,
　On the banks of the genial spring,
And put out its blossoms to cheer and bless,
　Like the breath from a seraph's wing.

She parted the clouds where the sun went down,
　With fingers like rosy shells,
And came, with the sweep of her hair so brown,
　Abloom with pearl-colored bells.
Clad in the folds of a blushing cloud,
　With a girdle of lilies white,

In tenderest beauty she over me bowed
    Till I trembled with wild delight.
"Oh, you have come back to your dear old home,
    To the hearts that have missed you so!
Our lives have drooped, and our joys are gone,
    Since you were laid under the snow.

"But you have come back with your love again,
    And gone is my desolate life:
I tramp in my joy on the weeds of pain,
    And laugh at the cold world's strife.
Put off the flowers of the pearly hue,
    The cloud with its foldings fair:
Your life in the angel-land is through;
    'Twas gingham you used to wear.
Come close to my side, and hear me tell
    How the months have dragged along,
And the moments rung with a ceaseless knell,
    But never a merry song.

"Come closer yet: I have dreamed before,
    And I fear I am dreaming now,
That you wandered back from the shadowed shore
    To our shadowed hearts below.
Oh, make me know I am wide awake,
    And you have come back to me!
Else to-morrow morn my heart will break
    'Neath the weight of its misery."
Her eyes looked sad, and she passed her hand
    Over my burning brow,
And a balm dropped off from the "Better Land,"
    As she said, "*You are dreaming now!*"

"When morning breaks, you will look for me
  Through the house, and among the trees;
But, darling, your eyes are too dim to see
  Far over the purple seas.
I watch, I wait by the gates of light,
  And my hand shall let you through,
When your days go down in the misty night
  To a land that is bright and new.
I would come back through the gate of pain,
  But only to comfort you."
"Oh, no!" I sobbed: " death has wrought you gain,
  And I can toil up to you."

GAZELLE:

A True Tale of the Great Rebellion.

I.

ERIE is peaceful as the breast
 Of childhood, ere the winds of sin
Fling snow-caps o'er its azure rest,
 And wreathe black shadows in between.
Our giant steamer splashes on,
 Crushing the ripples 'neath its tread,
Until the mirrored stars are gone,
 And the moon's shadow shakes its head.
Home! I will fade not from my heart
 As leagues of distance hurry in,
Holding haven and my soul apart,
 Nor promise we shall meet again.
The high, white walls I cannot see;
 But, mist as a spirit eye,
The parlor lamp-light shines to me,
 And speaks for home a mute good-by.
I dash into the dusky night,
 Night with her thousand pulsing stars,

Like Peris' eyes, leaning to sight,
   Atremble through the silver bars.

How hush and gentle is the Night!
   Her airs are toying with my hair
Like airy fingers, and her voice
   Lulls me to quiet like a prayer.

Gone through the holy gate at last,
   From boyhood into manhood free,
Ah! there are treasures in the past
   The future cannot give to me.
Some idols shivered in my face;
   Some dreams too rainbow-like to last;
The future is a mist-veiled vase;
   A broken goblet is the past.
Heaven gives us but one mother's breast,
   One term of childish innocence,
One time when mimicry is rest,
   And very fair is Ignorance.

Change rides upon the wings of Time,
   A regal artist, dumb and still,
Who visits God's remotest clime,
   And sculptures matter to her will.
She is no low, capricious hag,
   Whose labor is all objectless,
Who ruins empires, topples tows,
   And works alone for man's distress.
Look at the Past, and see how Change
   Has slowly cleared Progression's way:
The far Past is the midnight hour;
   The Present is a cloudy day

Ah! sighing over empires wrecked,
   And mighty nations cowled in gloom?
Error is mortal, and must die ;
   But Progress rises from its tomb.
Old Egypt spent her choicest strength
   To build herself a monument,
And perished as more perfect Greece
   Pushed high above her its ascent ;
Rome towered above her sister States,
   A glittering, ambitious queen,
Rich in the heirlooms of the past,
   And worth the world had not yet seen.

Europe, with all her nameless store
   Of cultivation, wisdom, pride,
Had marched through centuries of gore
   Before she reached the lighted side
Of God's humanity. Her veins,
   Though pure, have run barbaric blood ;
Her fair face has worn pits and stains ;
   But change wrought error into good.

We dwell in shadows like yon isles,
   So fondly brooded by the night,
Nested in waves. Sunshine beguiles,
   But we play blind-man in the light.

Those islands, with their purpling vines
   And cultured fields and cottage homes,
Where roaming wealth stops to drink wines,
   And the rest-searcher loves to come,
Have put another aspect on
   Since, when a smooth-faced boy, I came

Among their haunts to fish and hunt,
   And shoulder all my father's game.
The deer dashed there among the trees,
   And great snakes crept with slothful ease
Below where were the eagles' nests,
   Which looked like hay-stacks pitched in trees

Once when I sported in the wild,
   Glancing among the cedar shade,
I met in fright a red-man's child,
   With rosy shells and plumes arrayed;
A fresh flower on a withered stem;
   A last leaf on an autumn tree;
The last child of a boasted line
   Of strong-armed warriors was she:
Browned by the frosts, torn by the wind,
   'Mong graves above which Memory sighed,
Her father had remained to find
   A grave where his forefathers died.
His child remained, a dark-eyed maid,
   Graceful and timid as a fawn,
Whose jetty locks but half concealed
   A rich cheek like a dusky dawn.

"What was her fate?" Those waves may tell
   Which cry around yon rocky rim;
They rocked her to so deep a sleep,
   She ceased her weeping e'en for him, —
A white man in a hunter's garb
   One autumn, ere the winds grew chill,
Who came to kill time and rare game,
   And pitched his tent on yonder hill.

She watched him whistling through the wood;
    Her eyes grew bright, her ears bent low;
She loved him. Then she drank a cup,
    The softest name of which is woe.

How changed within a few brief years!
    Where were the Indian wigwams old
Are cottages and cultured lands,
    And rich fruits hang their globes of gold.

Moonlight and silence with the night!
    Lamplight and music with the fair!
Ah! bright cold things are yonder stars,
    Warm hearts are in the cabin there.

" A stranger, and how know I?" So:
    A cold heart cannot sing a song
And breathe life in it; so I know
    One heart glows warm among the throng.
Icicles are poor listeners,
    And so I know there must be two;
For one drinks in the melting wine,
    Silent as blossoms drink the dew.

She looks well: that's the major thing;
    Who looks well is well, I believe;
The face is chiselled by the soul,
    And if it would cannot deceive.
Most beautiful! How dewy sweet
    Her mouth! By heaven! I'd like the bliss
One could drink off from such pure lips
    In the enchantment of a kiss.

Her eyes are dark, and shrine a light
  Such as I've seen on wavelets glow;
Above them, wreathed in massive curls,
  Her forehead is a cliff of snow.
Her cheeks are pale, — too pale, perhaps;
  Sure she and Thought are bosom friends;
Her shape is matchless, and her form
  With every sway of feeling bends.
Her white hands dance upon the keys
  Like snow-flakes drifted by the wind,
As gusts of music rock her form
  And bear us pleasure undefined.

Another song! and I will hear,
  Though sung for dearer hearts than mine:
I am a worshipper of Song,
  And yield praise-offerings at her shrine.
Her white throat swells, and music rills
  Like crystal waters from a fount;
How many sounds her lips give out,
  Her fingers and the keys keep count.

  " World-strife or love-life —
    Which is the best?
  One is mad action,
    One is sweet rest.

  Armored with dollars
    One is a man,
  Wearing love's lily white,
    Be if one can!

Tinselled without or
 Golden within?
Hearts is the trump up —
 What can you win?"

A song with warm blood in its heart,
 Just coloring the dainty lines,
Tendrils which one might trace where fruit
 Hangs in rich clusters on strong vines.
That aged man with brow inclined,
 Like an o'er-fruited head of grain,
Looks proudly with a father's trust
 Upon the singer of the strain.
One young and handsome, nearer by,
 With calm blue eyes brimful of thought
Reminds me of a college friend,
 Save that life's earnest dreams have caught
In his deep eyes since he and I
 Learned as our learned professors taught,
And thought, " Once safely through the books,
 This world can vex our heads with nought."

How the heart clings to early friends
 It learned to love, ere earthly taint
Had left its blotches on the soul
 And made a mortal of a saint!
The memory of the pure young souls
 Which cluster round us in our youth,
Fades not; but, 'balmed within the breast,
 Through life remains life's sacred truth.

We talked of old times: then we traced
   Our swift feet to the present day,
Glanced at the future trustingly,
   And prophesied a sun-bright May
To stretch far in the coming years,
   With loves and joys, nor tears nor biers.

I asked him if, like me, alone
   He sought acquaintance with the world;
Or if some angel-hand had thrown
   His fortune where the loved and true,
With velvet hands and tender lips,
   And eyes of sunlight, ever threw
Evil and sorrow in eclipse.

" There is my sister, — do you know
   How dear a gentle sister is?
And how, like one inspired with truth,
   She finds life's radiant promises
For you, when your beclouded eyes
   Can only see the barren rocks
Towering before you, and your ear
   Hear nothing but the breakers' shocks?

" My father, too, discussing there
   With that Republican, has left
His Southern home and hundred slaves,
   Of over-opulence bereft.
He is surveying Northern minds,
   And Northern sentiment and strength, —
Style, mettle, courage, training, wealth:
   He wants to learn your breadth and length.

"What say you to a glass of wine?
   Wine is a warmer of the heart, —
A social creature : let us go
   And win the magic of her art."

We drank the foam-bells, and our souls
   Grew airy as the shining things :
They seemed to catch about our hearts
   And blossom into little wings.
We oped the parlors of our souls,
   And each one let the other in
To view the curiosities, —
   The little good, the legion sin.
Reader, step in : 'tis worth your time
   To look about the museum
Of a boy's heart, ere manhood's sun
   Has waked the better things to come.

The warm winds blow around the place,
   And wake sweet fancies, as in spring
The soft south winds in woodlands start
   The flowers which scent its viewless wing.
Ecstatic hopes abide with him,
   A troublous and capricious band,
Whose regal palace is his brain,
   Where Reason sits not in command.
A Quixote mentor comes betimes, —
   Some daring knight of windmill fame ;
Or, rather, he Quixote becomes
   In every thing except in name.
Blessed is he if Panza's tongue
   Drops proverbs in his wayward way,

And his experiences all turn
  To armor after each affray.

Some abstract goddess for a time
  Is ever sweeping past his eyes;
Soon to his highest joy he finds
  His goddess in some mortal's guise:
He offers that disordered realm,
  His heart, to her; she takes the throne,
Becomes a tyrant; he rebels,
  And sends her to Hate's frigid zone.

Next come a dozen, all at once,
  Who rapidly each other chase;
'Tis fun for them, but death to him, —
  The contest for the reigning-place.

Love-letters, tied with silken bands,
  Scented verbena and pink
Fly to him, little white-winged doves
  Which take him to the very brink
Of something serious, — something new, —
  When, lo! one comes with such a train
Of letter-escorts, that one view
  Kindles suspicion. Then he reads, —
"I send your letters back to you!"

Oh, what a trial to his pride
  To see those envelopes come back,
Their snow defiled, their tinsel dimmed!
  How many hours upon the rack

Of slow exertion was he strained
 To write his first love-letters! There
They are returned, — turned out of doors
 By his false-hearted May Adair.

He hurries off his lips a sigh;
 He wonders what may be the cause;
Consults his full-length looking-glass;
 Suspects it may have been some flaws
In his appearance; gives his hair
 Some extra curls, grows a mustache
And whiskers, buys a dagger cane,
 Scents with "West End," then makes a dash,
A finished dandy, deeming self
 Quite competent to right his wrong.
The lady surely will repent
 When he takes from the rosy throng
Of her companions some one else
 To-morrow evening to the ball,
And is the lion-beau of all
 The beaus which crowd the dancing-hall.

Hanging about the treasure-room
 Of Percy's heart are bold designs
Of coming hours, which he and Time
 Will finish up with shades and lines;
Gray fossils, too, in his young heart, —
 Idols, which once had pulse and thrill,
Have petrified within the breast,
 Which treasures them while they but chill.

II.

The air within these crowded rooms
    Is close and stifling: let us go
Out where the wind blows bland and free
    Upon the noble steamer's prow.
What a blest sense of quiet strength
    Comes o'er me as he hurries on,
When all things else seem fixed and still
    Except the waves he travels on!

The giant trees, with shaking arms
    Pointed at yonder timid stars,
Like Night's mock sentinels, are chained
    To one small foothold by the bars
Of fixedness. Those rippling waves
    Are fettered by the little brim
Of earth and rocks, pebbles and shells,
    Which lie around Lake Erie's brim.

My young friend's father, M. C. Earle,
    Suddenly joined us. I forgot
The "Auld lang syne" in his stern mien,
    And turned on him my eyes and thought.

He bore a dash of feudal pride
    Mingled with democratic grace;
But the hard soul which cowered the slave
    Had stamped its iron on his face.

A gentleman, and more a lord,
　　He bore himself. His stern gray eyes
Flashed 'neath a forehead broad and bold
　　Which sixty years had made world-wise.
He talked and walked, and queried much,
　　In manner *distingué* and suave,
Touching at length on themes of State,
　　And the great question of the slave.

This gentleman commenced his tour
　　Attended by a valued slave
Who owned his fullest confidence.
　　But, oh! what human soul can brave
Temptation to possess its own
　　Warm garment, when to choose is left,
To rise erect, or crouch and groan?
　　Does God book such intentions " theft "?

The master felt the lawless North
　　Had robbed him of his rightful chattel,
And in his heart he made appeal
　　To right that wrong by shock of battle.
" Was not the negro better South
　　Than in his native Afric jungle?"
He knew not if a Northman's head
　　Could solve that quiz without a bungle.

"Expediency is not the point
　　We are to touch," I said. " I ask you,
Would it be right for some strong prince
　　To claim you, seize you, and attach you,

And your descendants, for all time,
    To serve him, and his line of princes,
For no good reason, save this one,—
    'Tis better for you, sense evinces?

He knows your needs, he feeds you well
    On Ortelans and countless dainties,
Begems you and your palace halls,
    And makes you shining as a saint is.
'Tis plain, if you were not his slave,
    You could not taste his regal splendor:
Would it be better in the prince
    To keep you, or your freedom render?

Who first taught Africa the art
    Of slavery? The swart slave-trader.
She is the desolate domain
    Which his own avarice has made her.

The system of the great slave-hunts,
    Perfected by Mahommed Ali,
Showers sorrow over Nubia's plains,
    And stains with blood mountain and valley.
The dusky Nubians are forced
    To learn with skill the bloody tactics
Of war and cruelty. The Turks
    Have never let them rust for practice.

Not long ago I met a man,
    A Nubian, aged, but not stooping;
'Neath all his weight of age and wrong
    His step was firm, nor his head drooping.

His color was a dark, rich brown;
 His forehead full and broad and darkling;
Beneath his matted, hoary hair,
 His eye intense, deep-set and sparkling.

He told me in his simple way
 The headings of his life's long story.
I know in heaven he will be blest,
 If sorrow crowns the soul with glory.

The desert of the Upper Nile,
 Which smiles in here and there oases,
Has one which was his native home,
 Lit up with love and tender faces.
He had grown up to twenty years
 Securely in the desert village,
When one daybreak the cry was rung,
 "The Turks are out for slaves and pillage!"

Soldiers on foot, and wild Bedouins,
 And savages on dromedaries,
Cannon and lance, sabre and sword,
 The army, halting yonder, carries.
They call upon the village sheik
 To give the customary tribute
Of slaves. Would any volunteer?
 My hero offered the first minute.
"No," said the sheik. "Bring out my men!
 The sunset of to-morrow
Shall see us fighting with strong arm
 The foe with poisoned arrow.

Bring out my men! I will not give
    The slaves without a battle,
Bring out my men! Arrows shall fly
    Faster than cannon rattle."

Bravely they fought, meeting the foe
    Like demons, mad and daring:
Their courage was of small avail;
    For, vanquished and despairing,
The villagers crouched and turned back.
    My hero, faint and bleeding
From a flesh-wound, lay on the ground
    Nursing, and water needing.
His father stood beside him there,
    Defiant in his sorrow;
His mother bathed his wounds with tears,
    And trembled for the morrow.
"Surrender?"—"Never! I will die,
    And so shall they who love me!
Better be chained beneath the ground
    Than hear chains clank above me!"

He plunged an arrow in the breast
    Of the imploring mother:
Another pierced the weeping girl
    Bent o'er her bleeding brother.
He cast his eyes upon his boy,
    Holding the weapon o'er him,—
"Death's boat is waiting now for him;
    But I'll step in before him."
The arrow paused, but in the heart
    Of the old man. The dying

Gasps of the mother and her girl
  Were soft as love's own sighing.
He saw them die, he deemed it well,
  Deemed death well worth the trying;
'Twere better to die then and there,
  Than to be years in dying,
Prometheus-like, chained to the rock
  Of torture and abuses.
What are eternities of life
  If shut from life's sweet uses!

My Nubian like one dying lay
  Upon the sands, life's crimson
Fast flowing. All his hopes had fled,
  Except that death would come soon.
A Turk came up, and drew the dart,
  And stanched the red blood flowing.
He fainted: when he woke again
  Nile winds were o'er him blowing.
Tide, wind, and oar hurried them on
  Across the land of Pharaoh,
With ruined temples grandly set,
  Down to the mart of Cairo, —
A horrid passage, to which death
  Were but a bootless trifle.
The chafing wounds were nothing,
  If the soul could anguish stifle.
O God! it could not; but the tide
  Came like hot lava, seething;
Hope, happiness, and manly life
  In fiery madness wreathing.

He felt a man. His soul beat high,
  Leaping for native freedom:
Ah! not for that he journeyed now;
  Not from, but on to, Edom.

When in the great slave-mart he stood,
  He felt his wonted sadness
Burn, like the Afric lion caged,
  Into a hellish madness.
He beat his chains, and loudly dared
  A man around to buy him.
One grim old Moslem said he would
  (If they would firmly tie him)
Give just one hundred shinahs for
  That mass of bone and muscle:
He said, "I like the Nubian grit,
  But should not like a tussle."
They marched him to a palace gate,
  And then, his hands untying,
The Moslem sternly spoke to him:
  " 'Tis little use defying;
For here are slaves, who, with a word,
  Will lay a hundred lashes,
And leave you but a wounded mass
  Of blood and festering gashes."

"Lash me to death: I can but die;
  And, when all hope has vanished,
What is this thing you call life worth,
  From every pleasure banished?"

" Brave fellow," said the Mussulman,
" You are a slave no longer :
In manhood, and true nobleness,
    You are, I own, the stronger.
I'll send you to your Nubian wilds
    By the first boat that anchors ;
I will not own you when your chains
    Bespot your soul with cankers."

A light like morning's, broke by clouds,
    Poured through his heart its brightness ;
He could not speak, he scarce could see,
    So dazzling was the whiteness.
There, in the gleam, the desert shone
    Around the green oasis,
And there the little village sat
    Upon its verdant basis.
He saw against the sky the sheen
    Of palm-trees grandly gleaming,
He saw his friends with outstretched arms,
    And faces gladly beaming.
He saw his friends ; but calm and dead,
    With cold eyes fixed and beamless,
They lay unburied on the sands,
    In sleep, wakeless and dreamless.

What was there of that desert isle
    To make his heart beat lighter?
What was there in the wide, wide world
    To make his gloom grow brighter?
Alone, alone, O pitying God !
    Where mighty Desolation

Sits with white finger on her lip
    Amidst Fate's desecration.

He saw no more. His spirit sank,
    Oblivion's night came round him,
And softly to her Lethic breast
    With sable tresses bound him.

He tarried to gain health and strength;
    But, the good Moslem dying,
His children seized him for a slave,
    All promises defying.
Again they sent him to the mart,
    Now mute and broken-hearted,
Since that last, lurid gleam of light
    Like ghostly mist departed.

To view the city's teeming mart
    A Southerner was passing;
And, noticing the Nubian,
    Pronounced him most surpassing.
He paid his price. He owned the man,
    Now an enslaved American!

A desert space of thirty years,
    Of work and restless sorrow,
A wilderness of pain and sin
    Without hope for the morrow;
And yet his suffering was light
    Compared with many another:
He was his master's body-slave,
    And to him half a brother.

Yet pining, like an eagle caged,
 To breathe the air of freedom,
He longed to be a man once more,
 And not a thing of Edom.

For this he sought the polar star,
 (I met him on the morrow;)
And, though he wore no crushing chains,
 He bore a crushing sorrow.
He was alone: the wide world round,
 With his no heart was beating.
He journeyed to an unknown clime;
 But none would give him greeting.

" Your story moans like midnight winds
 Whistling through an eaves-spout.
Young hearts are tender, and young heads
 Are always leaving facts out.
Now listen while I tell a tale,
 True, simple, and pathetic:
Take out your handkerchief, and weep,
 If you feel sympathetic.

" In a menagerie I saw an orang,
 With nameless sorrow bowing his gray head;
He was imprisoned in a scanty whee-dang,
 Scarce larger than he wanted for his bed.
He looked as if to him life's crowning glory,
 His own God-given freedom, would be sweet;
And he sat sighing o'er the mournful story,
 That his oranghood was so incomplete.

"From a far realm a monster hand beguiled him,
    In life's June morning, when a bright career
Waited his doing. From high hopes he wiled him,—
    Home, love, and kindred, all the heart holds dear.
He forced the sire from seven little orangs,
    And a fond wife, who wrung her paws in grief,
And choked herself to death, before the whee-dang
    Which held her husband, as a last relief.

"Tears rilled his cheeks, he heard the wail of sorrow
    The little orangs gave, as on he sped:
He knew full well the dawning of the morrow
    Would see them orphans, with their mother dead!
And he — where would he be? Alone and lonely,
    Rocking, perchance, upon the ocean-wave,
Dreaming of bygone days, and hoping only
    In immortality beyond the grave.

"They hurried him aboard a splendid steamer,
    And placed his whee-dang in a sightly place,
Where men and women of uncouth demeanor
    Gathered, for pastime, to gaze on his face:
Insult and jesting he bore like a martyr,
    Was punched with canes, and knocked against the bars:
One hard old sailor, wicked as a Tartar,
    Regaled his nostrils with stump cent cigars.

"Next came sea-sickness, such a poor invention,
    The inventor ought to have been puked to death;
Or, in mild language, fed upon lobelia,
    And vomited till he threw up his breath.

The orang was alone through all his illness,
  His aching head bent on his pale, thin paw,
Harking for loved tones to sound through the stillness,
  And something of his agony withdraw.

" He reached, at length, a land across the ocean
  From his old home, where every thing was new,
And every thing was whirling with mad motion,—
  Wonders, inventions, humbugs not a few.
He had not learned the language; but an omen
  Seemed to foretell he'd be set whirling too,
For he was bought, and caged up by a showman,
  Whose brains could find him nothing else to do

" But circle round the country with a circus,
  And some wild animals, attached to please
Sage people, who, far better than the horse-fuss,
  Like captured animals to see and tease.
Hurried around from little ville to city,
  With such a set of reprobates he went,
Meeting no eye to give a look of pity,
  No joy blooms to appease his discontent.

" Artemas Ward, the showman, asked the orang
  If he supposed it would augment his joys
To have a mate live with him in his whee-dang,
  And by and by some little girls and boys.
Hope built her fires on the long-vacant altar
  Of that tried heart, and lit those sullen eyes
With love's own radiance. The marriage halter
  Put smiles upon his lips in place of sighs."

With the last line Earle marched away
    Contemptuous and conceited,
In thinking his Columbiad shot
    His foeman had defeated.
His gray eyes gleamed, as if a soul
    On fire was mutely gazing
About for something to consume,
    Such hate was in them blazing;
But not a word escaped his lips,
    His tongue was sly and cunning:
He hated Northmen, but was North,
    And weighty lessons conning.

The starry night had reached its noon,
    The boat dashed on, the wavelets darkled,
As fearful of the serpent wake,
    Which coiled and ran and foamed and sparkled.

Far in the dim horizon's brim
    Shine lights, as if a constellation
Had dropped, and broken all the stars,
    And multiplied illumination.
We near a landing, where we stop
    To give ourselves a needed Sabbath,
And go to church, and bless the Lord:
    Religion's is a jewelled path.
I'm fond of opulence; and yet
    When I have seen some jewelled brother
Fall o'er, and curse some lowly one,
    To reach the fingers of some other
Wearing a fortune in a ring,
    Wrung from tired hands, and cramped hearts
        breaking,

Who felt their wrongs, but knew no balm
  Except alone their silent aching,
I have grown murmurous, and lost
  Half the enjoyment of my riches,
And vowed I'd half as lief be there,
  As see my brothers in the ditches!

The Forest City! M. C. Earle
  Came out, restored, with Gazelle,
To ask us where we chose to go;
  So Percy chose the Weddell.

III.

Oh! it was beautiful, splendid,
   Virginia Cathedral to-night:
If the court-room of heaven had descended,
   And burst on our mortal sight,
I doubt if it would have been finer,
   I doubt if the holy air
Would have wafted an odor diviner
   Than the incense which floated there.
The carpet would fill with its velvet
   The arch of an Arab foot;
The hues of a purple sunset
   Were seen in the bishop's coat.
A stranger, I knew no strictures
   To fetter my dazzled eye;
And I gazed on the grand old pictures
   Of saints, in the world on high;
At the meek, sweet face of Mary,
   With tenderness and dread,
And wished that the hour would tarry
   A year o'er the holy head.

Dim eyes, ye begin to falter,
   Yet turn to yon radiant light,
Where, high o'er the blazing altar,
   A figure of Parian white,
With robes that are white and shining,
   And slender hands clasped o'er her breast.

And head like a lily inclining,
    Bends low to the praise of the blest.
She smiles and bows and listens,
    The image so white and cold,
High up where the soft clouds glisten
    With azure and silver and gold,
A form of such exquisite beauty,
    A face full of meekness and grace,
A villain would worship his duty
    To look at the smile on her face.
A thousand eyes, worshipful tender,
    Look up to the soul of the creeds, —
The virgin in exquisite splendor, —
    Then bow o'er the holy beads.

The organ was deep as the thunder
    Which rolls through the halls of the sky :
I opened my eyes in a wonder
    If Orpheus' spirit were nigh.
I thought, as the music went winging
    Its way through the gorgeous hall,
That the notes of an angel's singing
    Were mingled sweetest of all :
I looked for a mist of whiteness
    To float from the upper air ;
For eyes like the stars in brightness,
    And the sweep of sun-bright hair ;
For a mouth perfected in beauty,
    And a white throat swelled with song ;
I was only an entranced dreamer,
    A fool in a sober throng.

I know there are dark-eyed angels,
  Angels with midnight hair;
I know that the cheeks of sunset
  Are pure as the pink pearls are.

I turned from the angel faces
  So white in a mist of gold,
And thought there is dearth of graces
  Like these on earth to behold:
I turned from the bright immortals
  To the passionate Gazelle,
And thought, they are through far portals, —
  There is something sweet, as well,
Tender and warm and winning;
  Something a mortal may love
And worship, nor deem himself sinning
  By chaining a saint by his love.
All the way to the grand cathedral
  Her little hand lay on my arm;
All the way o'er the stony pavement
  Her feet mimicked mine to a charm;
And her voice was so low and bewitching,
  So earnest, and guileless of art,
Had I known her inventing a story,
  I'd vow it came straight from her heart.

I wonder if days which are coming
  Will bring me such bliss any more;
I wonder if days which are coming
  Will blush into love's rosy lore.

IV.

The sun arose. Young Morning swept
   The mist-wreaths from the autumn skies
With rosy fingers. Every thing
   Was splendid with autumnal dyes;
The morning air was rich as wine,
   And wheeled the pulses on their way
With fleeter swiftness. Still and chained
   I listened to the mighty lay
   Niagara hymned to the day, —
Music Omnipotence above
   Could measure, — tunes colossal souls
Hear with mute lips and heads hung down,
   As mourners list to funeral knells.

"A carriage, sir? a hack? a hack?"
"I've lived here twenty years and more;
I'll drive you round Goat Island, sir,
   For five good ones." — " A hack? for four!"
They swarmed like bees in clover-time,
   The hackmen, in the village-streets:
More greedy than are bottle-flies
   For blood, were they for golden sweets.

More wonders than my pen can tell
   Slid from their tongues at railroad speed;
Lies which had blossomed in the mouths
   Of their dead sires, and gone to seed,

And sprouted on their flippant tongues.
"A carriage?"—No! no chattering jay,
With eyes that look like two full moons,
　　Shall have my ears to twattle in
As long as Heaven spares me the boon
　　Of legs and feet. I'll walk and grin!

"Indian store." How many times
　　This superscription met my eyes
I will not mention, out of fear
　　You will declare, "The author lies."
I will affirm, I do *believe*
　　I saw twelve Indians hanging out
For store-signs, painted up to life
　　So true, you pause to hear them shout.

I went in. There was fancy-work,
　　"All made by Injuns," which would take
The famed tribes of America
　　Eternity to *learn* to make.
Beads in a thousand graceful shapes;
　　Vases all bloom with radiant flowers;
Bracelets of seeds and snowy quartz;
　　Crosses and beads for holy hours;

Sun-shades, and curious feather fans,
　　Which last I very much admired:
Indeed, if I'd been born a bird,
　　There's nothing I had more desired
Than to be skinned and dried and placed,
　　With wings all spread, in attitude

Most graceful, 'mong the airy plumes,
　　Secure from all things rough and rude,
And there receive the fond caresses
　　From lily hands that love expresses.

I strolled along the common way,
　　To gain the grandest points to see
The Falls, but found them all locked in
　　With a half-dollar for a key.
I paid it, saying to the man
　　Who took it, I presumed that he
Managed the Falls, and kept them up
　　In prime style for the world to see.

I walked along Goat Island's brim,
　　Turning off now and then to view
The beauteous shrubs, and varied flowers,
　　Which, just as Nature left them, grew.
'Twas strange the Yankee had let slip
　　The chance to set out something new.
The arbor-vitæ's feathery leaves
　　Were bowing to the toying breeze;
Clusters of snow-drops hid away
　　From notice in the rich green leaves;
The asters wore their royal robes
　　To be bound into autumn's sheaves.
Artists were thick as birds in spring,
　　All half becrazed to paint the wonder;
But could not get it natural,
　　Because they could not fix the thunder.

Ha! from this point the Falls
Burst on me in the full power of their terrible magnificence,
Near the summit
Like a precipice of emerald,
With the sun blazing upon it; below
Hurrying, plunging, breaking
Into countless myriads of foam-flecks,
White as the virgin snow on Jura's summit,
The waters leap into the gulf,
Where they half repose in the quiet of conscious strength.

Oh maniac waters!
Maddening my brain,
Dazzling, charming, terrifying,
Overcoming me, until I long to be taken to thy strong bosom,
And go down to repose where the rainbows lie asleep at thy feet.
God's masterpiece!
Were thy veil of mist removed,
I would turn away, and blind my eyes;
But I can look at that,
Then at the clouds bending o'er thee,
And bear thy grandeur.

There toils the "Maid of the Mist."
See the little steam-pipes throw out their tiny columns!
She challenges the disgorging ocean to combat.
How she bows to the billows!

Now she shakes her prow defiantly at the crazy
  flood, and hurries on.
Nearer, nearer,
Nearer, until she touches the hem of those awful
  foam garments!
She is dashed by the giant breath of the crashing
  avalanche,
And drowned by falling clouds,
As a hero storming a battlement,
Striving a time without advancing,
In whose face thunder a thousand cannon,
Is borne back by the press of numbers,
She turns, dashing the waves in defiance.

Terrific strength, set in a frame of calmness!
Only fools apostrophize thee!

V.

"A SPLENDID moon lights up the night,
Which charms me more than this hotel:
A garden on the British shore
I know, my girl, would please you more
Than aught you ever saw before;
The flowers are many, rare, and bright,
And silvered with such pearly light,
It could but be a charming sight:
   Come, go, Gazelle."

How pretty looked her pearly face!
She wound around her shining head
A cloud of azure hue and snow:
Sparkling above her peerless brow,
One brilliant threw its lucent glow
   Upon her banded hair.
A mantle hung with careless air
Around a form as full of grace
As many an one which holds its place
For ages in the Vatican,
Where pilgrim artists lightly tread
Among the marble, as if man
Had called the mystic gathering there,
And something struck them dead.

Can you think of a fancy that's sweeter,
   In this April-skied world of ours,

Than to dream yourself Adam in Eden,
   And walk through a garden of flowers
With an Eve for the lady you love best,
   And silver with moonshine the hours,
In lieu of the audacious sunlight
   Which ought to be barred from such bowers?

She grows on me still as the day beams
   On morning, though silent and cold;
And I fancy the sky bending o'er us
   Will warm into crimson and gold
A garden of flowers for confessing
   A love which has hid in the heart;
The flowers will take tongues, and, in telling
   The tale, act a beautiful part.

A sigh for me! do not grow angry,
   And say I am rude in my art,
To darken my picture, and tell you
   A truth out of place for the part.
I mention the thing as a warning
   To others who enter the bowers
For a like recreation, to bear this:
   They will gather no help from the flowers!

" Strangers are allowed to touch nothing,"
   Was posted beneath a bright light
At the entrance; I thought that the poster
   Should have the gold rule in his sight;
But that is a thing of tradition,
   It is not the text of to-day, —

A gem set in God's Holy Bible,
   Too precious for common display.

The walks were quite narrow : I drew her
   Closer to my side, as we wound
With the serpentine paths where they glided
   Round moss-vase and column and mound ;
There a moss-basket, hung from the branches,
   Held a plant of some tropical clime,
Whose slight, trailing branches were swinging,
   Like life on the finger of Time.

Here a vase which was wrought in the wildwood
   Was wearing as brilliant a crest
Of rare blooms as the head of a beggar
   Would wear in a diamond crown dressed ;
While statues looked out from the shadows
   Like spirits of beauty and love,
Such as burst on our brains on such evenings
   Wherever our footsteps may move.

A fountain kept trickling low music,
   Like fairy maids, ringing drop bells ;
A basin, with brim of fresh verdure,
   Was sprinkled with delicate shells.
Close by it a rustic seat waited
   With negligent ease to beguile ;
So we sat side by side in the shadow,
   To talk by the fountain a while.

" How deep the thunder of the water
   Breaks on this fragrant air !

Hast heard the story of the red chief's daughter,
  His pride and tender care,
Who drank the cup which the dame Custom
    brought her,
  And went to slumber there?
I know not where the mighty tide has borne her;
  But in their rocky cave
I can but think the water-spirits mourn her,
  And watch her grave.

" 'Twas an old custom of the red man, — wedding
  A virgin to the God
Of vast Niagara each year, for shedding
  Mercies where'er they trod.
I dream there may be trees in this old wood
  Which shrine the Falls,
Whose leaves cast lots for who should wear the
    flower bands,
  And wrap in the foam fall.
    'Twas long ago. But here are trees primeval,
Which, had they tongues, could speak
  Of other years, and many a vanished evil,
Till thy light heart would break."

She raised her own, which on my arm was lying,
  And placed it near my hand:
" Tell me the story; I would fain be sighing
  Under thy mystic wand.
I long to weep; I am heart-sick of smiling
  On smilers not a few.
Something soul-deep may chance end in beguiling
  Tears, — tears for you."

LEGEND OF THE WHITE CANOE.

Like a white foam-cap from the sea
    Upon the emerald water,
The white canoe rocked restlessly
    To win the old chief's daughter.

The brightest flowers which Summer's hand
    Had sprinkled o'er the island
Were woven in a rainbow strand,
    And chained the white boat to the strand.

Upon the shore an Indian maid
    A solemn prayer was breathing.
Ah! it was she in white arrayed,
    And snowy blossoms wreathing,

Who was to row the white canoe
    Over the leaping river,
Down where the mighty Manito
    Was waiting to receive her!

Her father came. She hung her head
    Like a rain-laden blossom:
"To-night will be the first," she said;
    "Your child has left your bosom."

He knit his brow, he stroked her hair,
    Speaking a word of cheering:
"Thy mother's shade comes on the air;
    Her bosom thou art nearing.

"Who will twine round the aged oak,
    The hero of the forest,
When shivered by this thunder-stroke?
    Oh, thou, Great Spirit, knowest!

Young maidens bound her tiny feet
    With plaited bands of flowers,
And named the trembling girl complete
    To grace Manito's bowers.

They placed her in the white canoe,
    With many a farewell laden,
And called two spirit-braves to row
    Their offering to Aidenne.

The boat shot off into the flood,
    Not 'mid a wail of sorrow,
But calm and still the whole tribe stood,
    And thought of Menah's morrow.

See! what is that which shoots in view
    From yonder hazel bushes?
The poor old chief in a canoe,
    To join the white boat, rushes!

The two canoes are side by side,—
    The father's and the daughter's:
They ride together o'er the Falls,—
    Where, O ye maniac waters?

To a mystic, awful grave,—
    A home in the Summer-land,

Where olive and myrtle wave,
   And Love knows no broken band.

It is sweet, with a sinless soul,
   To pass from a thorny crown;
To be set in the shining goal,
   With no strife of winning known.

He tastes not the bridge of sighs
   Which leads from the dungeon cell
Who youthful and sinless dies:
   It was well for Menah, — well!

The sun of childhood is its mother's face;
   The glory from it warms and blesses all.
If it go down, what can light up its place?
What coming moon the blackened void efface?
   The child goes crying through a crape-draped
      hall
   To find its mother, but finds none at all;
Then wakes to this sad truth, — the Holy One
Through all Time's changes gives us only one.

I know this truth; for, when a merry child
   Of scarce four summers, my young mother died.
I saw them take her, with a brain half wild,
And bury her where flowers and sunshine smiled
   Around her; but her lips and heart were cold;
   Still and unswaying was the dear head's gold;
   And some one told me years would make me
      old,

And lay me in the ground like her, before
I ever could sleep on her bosom more.
Ah, bitter truth! what could I do but cry,
And call her back, and ask my father why
She left her baby when she loved it so,
And it would cry each coming hour to go?

He gave me to a nurse of night's own dye,
With coarse high voice, and darting jetty eye,
And uncouth air, and bade her give me care
Such as I needed. O my friend! despair
Comes with such changes, more than soul can bear.
To live one moment in a blooming place,
Then in a desert where there's not a trace
Of all the richness which you deemed your own,
Is a transition which but once is known.

I, half unthinking, kissed away a tear,
   Which, like a jewel, glittered on her cheek;
And bent my lips to speak some word of cheer,
   And kissed her over; but she did not speak.
I grew more bold, and on her coral lips
   I placed one, warm, and longer than the rest:
That time I felt her rosy finger-tips
   A little closer on my own hand pressed;
And then the feelings of her heart I guessed,
And drew her willing head upon my breast.

Gazelle, if you will love me, by yon stars
   Which burn forever on the brow of night,
I pledge a love, which, while their silver cars
   Wheel on, shall never turn from you its light.

"Love you? I will; and life will be a draught
  Richer than Cleopatra's, at her feast
For Antony, with holier motives quaffed,
  Not striving to be greatest, but the least."
Then warm and trustingly she laid her hand
  Full in my own, and freer fell her head
Upon my bosom. "Love and Truth shall stand
  The guardians of my soul where'er I tread."

Then, like a shadow flitting o'er a brook,
  A raven thought ran darkening through her
      eyes:
What is it, love? "Oh, if he would not brook
  Your Northern sentiments in a son's guise!
I tremble, Adrian, I know him well, —
  His firmness, pride, his plans for his Gazelle;
And — bend your ear — there's treason at the
      South!
I tremble, — this I fear I should not tell;
Caution keeps putting finger on my mouth, —
  My father is a statesman; and I know
By floating straws, by little words I hear,
  Which way the currents of opinion flow;
And that the blood-red feet of war are near:
  My father's business — more I will not tell;
A sense of filial duty would rebel.
  God grant us this! — our lovings prosper well."

"Our souls are free, Gazelle; no tyrant hand
  Can ever shake a chain of bondage there; .
Wear this slight ring, — this little golden band, —
  And your white hand will grow more purely
      fair.

Now kiss me, sweet, the first time in your life, —
There is a breath of something on your lips
Which maddens while it charms, my plighted wife,
And throws all tasted pleasures in eclipse.

The moon is waning: we must leave these bowers, —
Sacred to memory through all coming hours."

VI.

Strange prophecy ! what evil can she mean
  Which hastens to o'ertake this prosperous land?
What grim-faced monster has the young girl seen,
  Wrapped in gore-clots, behind light language,
    stand?
I wish I could believe her splendid eyes
  Can sometimes blunder when she reads the heart;
  But, no! she is no bungler in the art
By which she says some crow-black error flies
  To feed upon the nation.

                    Swift we go
Over Ontario's waters, deep and still
  And beautiful as e'er a sunset glow
Lit up with crimson glory; Nature's will
  Worked grandly when she wrought this crystal
    chain
Of sea-like lakes, and rivers marching free,
  And sent them thundering onward to the main
Across her garden-spot, — America.

The steamer dashed the waves away in pride,
Like chuckling babies clinging to her side;
And they ran off, and in a shimmer died.
  I sat alone among the many there
Upon the deck, and looked into the clouds
  Piled round the sinking sun in grandeur rare,

While my poor brain raised castles in the air,
And saw the friends I love, without a care
Look through the windows, growing saintly fair,
Till some great cloud wrapped them from me in
    shrouds.
Evening leaned out, as looking after Day,
A globed pearl on her bosom. One by one
The scattered passengers had dropped away
To seek the wing of slumber. I alone
Remained, and mused how mighty forces play
Upon men's destinies. One little day
Had put new meaning in my life. The wine
Of loving words had drunked me. Now I felt
As if the strength of Hercules were mine.
What if life's storms about my head should pelt?
Gazelle and love and promises were mine ;
And yet a deep, vague darkness troubled me
About the heart, lit by no Pharos gleam,
Whose shapeless features might come yet to be
A joy or sorrow, or an empty dream.

Something said, "Bare thy brow, and hurry on,
    Nor stop to dream of coming Misery.
She follows those who beckon, — hurry on,
    And dream not when you sail a dangerous sea.
List to the engine, with its heart of fire
    Combating with those giants, Time and Space,
Like a strong man whose labor meets desire,
    And bears him on a hard-wrought earthly race."

    It is midnight, and the glimmer
        Of the ghostly Northern fires

O'er the water sends a shimmer
    As each phantom light expires;
Then they rise in shining stairways,
    Such as many a martyr trod
Upward through the crystal gateway
    Leading to the smiles of God.
One by one the streamers shaded
    With the darkness, growing dimmer,
Till the conflagration ended
    In a scarce distinguished glimmer.

Then I saw a black cloud, brightening,
    Dash against the patient stars
With a forehead gilt with lightning
    Spread across in lurid bars.
Piles on piles, like growing mountains,
    Snow-capped, and by whirlwinds torn,
Came the clouds, like flying fountains,
    Onward by the fleet winds born.

Then I heard the water, waking,
    Shudder as in deep despair,
As it heard the monster shaking
    In the vaulted halls of air;
But the steamer walked a true line
    Onward in her destined course;
And I thought the throbbing engine
    Labored with a mightier force;
Bore our prow up to the gleamer,
    Where it broke in hills of foam,
Bearing down the gallant steamer
    With a long and labored groan;

Then receded for a brief rest,
    Like a wolf flung from the sides
Of a giant of the forest,
    Which its puny power derides.
What a scene of awful glory!
    Talk you of the thundering Falls?
I can tell a wilder story,
    Charming when it most appalls.
Stand with me, and feel our shell fall,
    Crashing, from a mountain swell, —
Nothing but a hollow foot-ball,
    Which the Storm-King tosses well.
Crash and hiss, and on in thunder
    Rush the demons for their prey;
You must feel there is a wonder
    Greater than Niagara.

Driven by the falling deluge
    To the cabin, there I met
Ashen faces, asking refuge
    If God's mercy saw them yet.
All were frightened out of senses;
    Many said, " 'Tis for my sin
That the holy Lord dispenses
    Troubles, which but just begin."
Then they vowed, if he would spare them,
    Life as holy as a saint,
Virtue's jewels, they would wear them,
    Hiding every earthly taint.

I could feel the danger waning,
    Feel the tempest taking flight;

And I thought the good boat gaining
    Safety ere the morning light.
Nature, kind and ever loving,
    Sent her helpless children aid:
Almost always her reproving
    By her kindness is repaid.
Easily the boat was moving,
    And all fear was wholly laid.
"Danger over!" cried the captain;
    "All the tempest's wrath is spent!
To your feet, and act like sane men!"
    Faster, faster, on we went.

On we plunged into the darkness!
    All below was liquid darkness!
All above was misty darkness;
    All around us thickest darkness!
Then a crash! and then a shrieking
    Rose from all! The steamer reels;
What mad devil has been wreaking
    Vengeance on her giant wheels?
"She is going!" shouts the captain
    In a voice of hoarse command;
"Man the boats, boys! work like true men,
    As you hope to get to land!"

Crowding, waiting, praying, cursing,
    Asking aid, but all in vain;
Gathering here, and there dispersing
    Like thoughts in a crazy brain.

Where was she, Gazelle? She left us
    When we thought the danger past,

Saying we had better rest us,
  Brooded by sweet Peace at last.
In the long-boat? in the life-boat?
  No, not with the surging throng.
"To her state-room like a thought float!
  Burst the door; die or be strong!"
In my circling arms I caught her,
  Yet asleep, and wrapped my cloak
Round her form. By Heaven! I brought her
  Out in less than one heart-stroke.

Filled to brimming was the boat-room,
  Not a foothold left for me:
So I turned to find my own doom
  In the darkness and the sea.
She was safe; for I had cast her
  In the midst of throbbing life,
My hard fate at least went past her,—
  I could meet the coming strife.

I with two or three old sailors
  Stood upon the sinking craft.
"Get some planks! we're not bewailers:
  Who knows where the waves will waft?"
Now that life and joy were pending,
  I felt strong to do and dare;
If my life must have an ending,
  'Twould be nobler than despair.
Off we went, bold undertakers;
  Sunk the ship with one wild roar,
Like the sound of countless breakers
  Dashing on a rocky shore.

Some lost wretch went drifting by me;
   Little matter who, thought I:
Such a night as this we know none;
   But I cannot let her die.
Till daybreak I toiling bore her
   With me, keeping both afloat,
Her wet ringlets sweeping o'er her
   Shoulders and her choking throat.

Weaker, weaker, each endeavor
   Which I used to float for life,
Every white wave answered, " Never
   Shall you two survive the strife ! "
Morning folded back the curtain
   Hanging o'er the storm-rocked world;
In the distance, I was certain
   Something like black smoke-wreaths curled.
What strange strength the mere thought gave me !
   Worked my hand like oaken oar,
Hoping that a boat would save me
   And the slender girl I bore.

First I saw a towering steam-pipe
   Set in the horizon's brim;
Watching still, I saw a snow-white
   Steamboat grow upon its rim.
Joy! She spied us! She was heading
   For us, strugglers with the sea,
Like a mighty angel shedding
   Radiance over misery.

Then I vainly strove to waken
   Her I bore upon my breast;

But her senses slept unshaken,
  And her head hung on her breast
Like a dead bird's. Not mistaken?
  No: O God! Gazelle I pressed!
How, oh, tell me, came she floating
  Over peril such as this?
Had I all that time been boating
  Her o'er Lethe's dark abyss?

We were all again together,
  Steaming o'er the waters blue,
Thanking fate for sunny weather,
  With no threatening cloud in view.

VII.

Down the St. Lawrence, by the Thousand Isles,
   Round which the waters laugh in quiet glee,
And even sunshine bursts in brighter smiles,
   And foliage bright as earth can give beguiles
To hang above the waters whisperingly,
   Waving the birds.

                Softly the Regis bell
Rang out its music from the high church-tower,
Which stood, like a tall watch, to mark the place
Where sat the little village at its feet,
Fearful God might forget to show his grace
To such humility. Each vesper hour
That iron-tongue rang out: "Here are we, God;
Pass this way with thy mercies, not thy rod;
Thy dusky children pray with the great bell."
A French Canadian told the story well,
With nod and gesture running through the story
Swift as the perfect on the road to glory.

THE BELL OF ST. REGIS.

Long years ago, when Time and I were younger,
A Jesuit priest came to yon Indian town;
Mystic his air, a real language-monger,
He rent their myths, and tore their heaven down

Above their heads; then builded up his own,
And bade the red man strive for it alone.

He reared a church, and set his men collecting
Furs for the purchase of the magic thing,
Making strange noises, how was no detecting,
Beneath the shadow of the steeple's wing;
The deer would hear its ringing miles away,
And birds rock to its music in the spray.

The furs were gathered and sold, and all accruing
Was sent away to France to buy the bell.
By some mishap, a British cruiser, viewing
The hard-earned prize, presumed it would be well
To take this bell, and send it to a colony;
The good 'twould do would compensate the felony.

O luckless Deerfield! Grim Abaddon waited
    To work his mission in a gory way.
The bell rang from thy church-tower fated! fated!
    But, oh! ye wist not that a transient day
Would work such agonies. Thy worshipped God
Spares not a single sinner from the rod.

He has no favorites whose misdeeds he winks at,
    And shields from justice with a partial hand;
He wakes in deep humility who thinks that
    His ways are God's, and for all men must stand.
Too many think the same, whose degradation
Will brook no meddling at regeneration.

The Jesuit woke the warriors of St. Regis:
    He bade them in the name of God go out

Under the banner of the stern Nemesis,
    And try, by arms, to bring the right about.
"Scalp, slay, and burn, nor spare the sinning people;
Shout till the stolen bell rocks in the steeple!

"Wake up their babies with your yells infernal,
    And hush their crying with your scalping-knife!
Despatch a legion to the land eternal,
Where God will wreathe hell's tortures on a life
Which cannot wane; while with our mighty bell
We'll praise him that he doeth all things well."

The village clock struck one. The lingering moon-
    light
Dropped down behind the forest on the hill,
Lighting it here and there. What fiends has mid-
    night
Left in those shades, so stealthy, grim, and still?
Noiseless as shadows, fierce as imps of hell,
They come to kill and burn, and get their bell!

They stole upon the village, wrapped in dreaming,
    Its bright eyes shut in unsuspecting rest.
It wakes to catch the tomahawk's swift gleaming,
    And murderous eyes and dancing warriors' crest;
Stalking through every house like crazy Death,
Hunting for blood and pain and fluttering breath.

O Indian torture! language cannot name you,
    O savage man, omnipotent in sin!
God, your Creator, can't do less than blame you,
    And think he would not make your like again.

"Whatever is, is right:" so says a teacher,
And human suffering is a lying preacher.

The ancient Scythians were not half as gory
  In scalping victims as these modern men;
Nero would blush at many a red man's story,
  And think Death's cruel arts aroused again
In far more cunning hands than his were, when
He tasked himself in torturing Christian men.

Day broke in silence, all of life had vanished;
  The writhing victims to the smiling skies;
The prisoners, from their homes and kindred banished,
  Followed the victors, bearing off their prize
To where it now swings in the old church-tower,
A relic of the red man's former power.

The village faded on the gliding waves,
  And emerald foliage, laughing in the light,
Shut from my misty sight the sombre graves,
  Hung with the dark of human nature's night.
Progression is man's savior, born and grown
  In deep humility. It gathers strength
From agonies. 'Twill gain a spotless throne
  And rule a sinless populace at length.

Away, O moralizing thoughts! Go guest
  With those two fossils in "Kentucky jean"
And stove-pipe hats, — sojourners from the West,
  Who nurse for modern things their deep disdain.

They do not like that lady's sweeping skirt:
　　One tells the other, in a crusty way,
"Tread on it! I'll not keep on the alert
　　To humor folks in such uncouth display."
One pokes the other in the ribs, and says,
　　"Do you suppose that dashy lady there
Is that man's *wife*? I've heard of awful ways
　　Some men get in." — " I dun' know as I care,
So Bulah Ann and me keep sailing fair."

"I wish my saucy Jake was here to thrash
　　That sleek, conceited dandy coming by,
Rigged like a trooper. He shall cut a dash
　　With my cane's help. Don't laugh, now, if you die!"
The old fox looked; the dandy strutted by,
　　His eyeglass searching o'er the charming shore:
"Pride must come down! the text applies to you!"
　　The cane slid out, and he sprawled on the floor.
"Tut, tut! old boy, how do you like the view?
　　That tool of yours you carry for your eyes
Has treated you to this profound surprise:
　　You stumbled on my cane; 'tis mighty mean,
'Twill carry an idee that you're green!"

The warm sun sparkles on the sapphire waves,
　　The cottagers wave to us from the shore,
And now and then a swell of music laves
　　The soul, and leads it back to memories yore.
How sweet it is to let one's self forget
Each craven fear, each foolish, fond regret,
The foes we shun, the dangers which beset,
And dream that none are worth man's notice yet!

VIII.

A SLENDER girl, wan-faced and eager-eyed,
    Of scarce ten summers, with a rosy child
Too weighty for such arms, passed me, and sighed
    In weariness. The baby crowed and smiled,
And loved the tender care the wee thing gave;
But she was thoughtful, womanly, and grave.
Whose charge was she? — she, but a tiny thing
Just large enough to play and romp and sing,
And flit about on childhood's glittering wing.
    I asked her. " None but heaven's," she sadly said,
And dropped her dewy eyes, and hung her head.
" You are a little child, fit for a pet
For your mamma to love and fondle yet."
" I am a nurse-girl for this baby; he
Is a rich baby; all is in degree;
I am too poor for love; I never knew
How scant a pittance of true love I drew
Until I saw how he is loved. Oh, gold
Buys time, and love for gold is sold."
" God's love shines through our parents. Have you none
That you bear burdens shirked from shoulders grown?
Nature did not intend children to bear
The part you take in vigilance and care."

"Father nor mother, sir, I never knew;
'Tis said rum burnt one's heart out, and he grew
Wicked and vile as aught you ever knew;
And mother grew as white as yonder foam
Flecking the waves which round that islet roam;
That when he died my mother did not weep,
But, like a frozen lily, dropped to sleep.
It seems I was forgot, left out of place,
Set down by chance, upon the blinding race
Called life, — I'm sure I know not why.
I work, you see; for I must work or die.
Whose charge am I? 'Tis pitiful to ask;
To find an answer is an angel's task."

Her eyes grew sadder, and a heavy tear
Dropped on her hand. I told her she was dear
To God and me, and bade her keep good cheer;
When a shrill voice called out, "Vernette, come here,
And bring the baby! You must keep him near."

IX.

The deck was swarming: every eye was turned
　Upon the rapids breaking on our sight.
The steamer hurried, as if fear she spurned,
　And entered danger with a wild delight.
　The azure waters seemed to take affright,
And changed to surging snow, so shining white,
'Twas life or death, no rescue from a wreck.
We breathless watched upon the rocking deck,
Nor hoped nor feared, but viewed the peering rocks,
And caught the spray, and bore the grating shocks.
We trusted fully in the magic skill
Of mind o'er matter, — matter chained by will.
All steam shut off, four stalwart men to steer,
The lithe craft bounded like a hunted deer.
The great waves broke in heavy showers of rain:
She shook it off, and leaped the flood again,
And cleared the danger. Then we silent smiled,
And at each other looked; then spoke and smiled.

Three times alike we ran the crazy tide,
　And all but the La Chine were safely passed;
'Twas said we were to have an Indian guide
　To steer us through that stormiest and last.
No hand but his was true enough to hold
So many lives, nor lose one from his fold.

From yonder little hamlet, a canoe
Rowed by two boys comes leisurely in view.

How gracefully it skims the rippling blue!
In the low stern, a mystic figure sits,
   With folded arms, and plume-decked head inclined:
His look is such as royalty befits, —
   A royal person and a royal mind;
Shown by his attitudes and chaining glance,
They are effects, and not the tricks of chance.
The boat came up: the captain waved his hand,
The steamer slackened at his quick command;
The Indian pilot scaled her dripping side,
And we sped on to meet the dangerous tide.

Far up the stream it sent its angry voice,
Hissing and raging over sunken rocks,
Our craven hearts were left no other course
Than to rush on, and dare the shivering shocks.
We all drew back: there was no place to go;
Water behind, before, around, below.
Batisté grasped the wheel. 'Twas he alone,
With hands of iron and a heart of stone,
Who dared the breakers, as he long had known
His power most potent. It was grand to see
How much a hero one strong man can be.
All eyes forgot the danger of the hour,
And turned on him, — a miracle of power.
He held the cumbrous mass of floating wood
True in the channel serpentine and rough;
And, in a little space, she upright stood
On the smooth wave. Oh! it was grand enough
To awe all souls. But when the silence broke,
" Three cheers for old Batisté!" smote the air;
And the tall steam-pipes sent the curling smoke
Over the waters and the landscape fair.

X.

The gray church-towers of Notre Dame
  Rise high into the sunset's gold,
Dispensing reverence by its name,
  Its aspect grand, its memories old.
I thought how, centuries ago,
  A poor girl-mother and her child
Lay in a stable. Did she know
  The destiny, the romance wild,
Which time and ignorance would throw
Around her? No, a crimson glow
  Would have burned up her dove-like brow
  Could she have seen the distant now.
For she was pure and wise and good,
And poor withal, and understood
  The ways in which Magnificence
  Glitters at Poverty's expense.

The fat-faced priest, with snowy hands
  And costly robes ; his livid brother,
Ground down by working others' lands,
  To buy him many and many another,—
Were contrasts which a holy heart
  Would shrink in horror from producing,
And call the framer of such art
  Not Heaven-sent, but God-abusing.

  No rushing and bustling,
  No pitching and tussling,

No crowding and jostling,
No smothering babies,
No uncertain maybes,
No changing valises
And hustling back;
For here the police is
To see that such species
Are kept in the forward track,
And not switched off to run back.
Order, even at the landing of a steamboat,
(To the honor of Montreal read this last note.)

Rocking along the streets in a fine carriage,
   Up Great St. James to the St. Lawrence Hall,
I swore I would not wealth again disparage,
   But take such favors as on me might fall,
   And praise my luck, and find no fault at all.

XI.

In the fragrant mists of the morning
    Nature is sweetest to me,
With dew-gems and rose-cloud adorning,
    And music of bird minstrelsy;
The leaflets look daintily varnished
    By fairy hands during the night;
All the flowers which the daytime has tarnished
    Are dusted and freshened and bright.

The clouds are more brilliant and fleeting,
    The waters run on in the light,
And the heart cannot choose but give greeting
    With pulses of bounding delight.
My heart was a mirror reflecting
    All beauty and joy and unrest,
And love was agreed in directing
    A ride to the mountain's blue crest.

Gazelle, — shall I call her my angel? —
    Transparent and trusting and free,
She yielded her lips, my evangel,
    So sweetly, completely, to me.
She smiled when I called her my treasure,
    And loaned me her dear little hand;
She ventured that love was a pleasure
    The *heart* of Divinity planned.

Frown not, chaste Diana! my beauty,
    Like pure mountain-snow, has a heart:
You will own, if you follow your duty,
    Love a most intuitional art.
" You think her not coy enough?" Give me
    The freedom of taste, — I'm a man, —
A woman would have her, believe me,
    Conduct on a different plan;

Would have *her*, when icily viewing
    The scenes she has been passing through,
Be saucy, and hard of subduing, —
    She'd *plan* what *she* never would do!
Male authors make heroines decent
    And gentle and sweet in their loves;
But women's are always on ill bent,
    And head one, no odds how he moves.

I never could see the completeness
    Of kissing finaled by a box
On the ears. All the mystical sweetness
    Takes wings, and flies after the knocks.
If you venture a name of endearment,
    It is not very pleasant, if " cool,"
To be told that your breath is all misspent,
    And you an improvident fool.

O shade of dead Xantippe! ladies
    Who court on this kind of a plan
Are the ones who turn home into Hades
    To torture some innocent man.
I felt not at all like complaining
    Because she'd not knocked off my hat;

I felt not at all like disdaining
    Her commendable hate for combat.

The glorious view from the summit
    Was like a choice canvas unfurled,
Whose scenes by some magic were sunlit,
    And culled from the wealth of the world.
In the distance the evergreen mountains
    Repose like dim realms of the sky,
Over which the soft clouds pour in fountains.
    On either hand, plains with plains vie;
Rich farms, like gay counterpanes, spreading
    Their harvests and fruits in the sun;
While *anear* the broad river is treading
    In glittering majesty on.

How I longed for an empire of glories
    Made up of such landscapes as these,
Filled with genii, like old Moslem stories
    Whose mission was princes to please!

By a wish I'd have set their swift fingers
    Framing a gem palace for me,
That would look like a bright dream which lingers
    And turns to sweet reality.

In the land where strangely and completely
    Reals and ideals are blended,
Loves offerings will shape, oh, how sweetly!
    And vain aspirations be ended.
What mysteries charming and tender,
    Which flee from our curious eyes,

Are stored for our spirits to render
   Away in the blue of the skies!

I wonder if deep aspirations
   Will bring us the things we require;
Or still, as a just compensation
   For acts, we grasp what we desire.
I know there will be joy in living
   Unknown in this bee-hive of pelf;
There will not be the lending or giving,
   But each man must work for himself.

Then princes with lordlings for servants
   In earth-life will be nothing more,
With no hirelings to satiate their slight wants,
   Than the people they governed of yore.
A day or two hence, yonder city
   Will gaze herself drunk on a Prince
Who is not over-brilliant or witty,
   But common as two-shilling chintz.

And yet there's a crown hanging o'er him,
   The boy who is coming this way;
There is royalty's power just before him,
   And souls for his sceptre to sway.
To-morrow he guests with yon city:
   Its heart is a-flutter to-day;
It is doing its best to look pretty
   In every conceivable way.

It will show itself well in the evening,
   Bedecked for the Prince's grand ball;

It will flit on an azure and gold wing
  In the dances at St. Lawrence Hall.
I envy the fellow, by Cupid!
  One species of trophy he'll win:
Ladies, be he never so stupid,
  Will love him, nor dream of the sin.

Well, we stoic men must endure it,
  And pet our Havana cigars,
And think that a brief time will cure it,
  Since princes must keep in the bars
Of royalty. Luck to their heartaches!
  And luck to their coming of sense!
Good luck to our laughs at their mistakes,
  And boxed ears in sad consequence!

XII.

To-day, to-day, the city stands
    A-tiptoe for a promised joy, —
A silly child, with upraised hands
    To grasp an over-gilded toy.
Triumphal arches span the streets,
    Triumphal arches span the quays,
Blooming with all the floral sweets
    Summer's and Autumn's wealth displays.
The steamer, white as mountain snow,
    With England's colors on her mast,
Her deck with gayety aglow,
    Sails in. The Prince has come at last.

The multitude, like ants or bees,
    Swarm round his carriage everywhere;
Not satisfied with what it sees,
    Impatient almost to despair.
Strange nature! Insects swarm as well
    As mortals round a royal worm:
A thousand years, and who can tell
    Which was the Prince, and which the worm?

He is an inoffensive boy,
    But a most royal mother's son.
Honor him; feed her heart on joy;
    Much good for England she has done!

XIII.

The festal hall outvied the night
  In softened splendor : 'twas as though
The stars were grouped which shone most bright,
  And festooned with a fixed rainbow,
To hang within the gorgeous hall.
  So beautiful the chandelier,
The light blazed on the glittering wall
  Above, so like a sun drawn near
The huge star wrought of diamond glass.
  Rich vases filled with rarest flowers
Attract the dancers as they pass
  Like Moslem saints in Houris' bowers.
A pyramid of roses there
  Rises from shoulders dimpled deep,
Bearing a head and face so fair
  In wanton beauty, it will keep
A heart-niche, though you bid it go,
  And with unhallowed fancies sleep :
A thing of beauty dies not so.
A group of drooping lilies bend
  Above a Parian angel's face,
As if heaven deigned its aid to lend
  To make more beautiful the place.
Rare flowers perfumed the luscious air,
  Such as are coaxed by fingers white
For years, with tenderest of care,
  Before they tremble into sight.

Wild poems carved in marble forms
   Held niches round the beauteous hall;
Forms never pelted by life's storms,
   Sweet faces free from death and fall;
Beings which age nor time can change,
   Immortal more than others are;
Something the world cannot estrange
   From beauty, nor its jarrings mar.
A thousand years may roll away,
   And changes rock the yielding earth,
And yet those thrilling dreams in clay
   Are just the same as at their birth.
Nothing was wanting to complete
   The pompous grandeur of the ball;
All things were for the young Prince meet, —
   The courtly people and the hall.
How Fashion triumphed! Charming belles
   Were thick as butterflies in June.
Crapes, satins, tissues, brocatelles,
   Fluttered and rustled to each tune;
Great diamonds flashed on moony pearls,
   And ruby laughed at amethyst;
Papas paraded pretty girls
   With hearts unpledged and lips unkissed.

Gazelle, my young azalea flower,
   Hung lightly on her father's arm, —
The Venus of that evening hour, —
   To other eyes than mine a charm.
Her heavy hair, wreathed into curls,
   Looped from one shoulder by a wreath

Of lucent emeralds and pearls.
　Her dress was satin, underneath
A robe of lace, which more subdued
　The mere tint of its viewless green;
Such dainty blendings I have seen
　Upon a lace-wing's wing, when viewed
Before a glowing lamp.　Glide on,
　O thrilling music!　Make soft eyes
Glow radiant as a June day-dawn;
　Make mournful lips forget to sigh,
And feet with hurrying measures fly,
And Sorrow flash in Pleasure's dye.

"Imagination rules the world,"
　Napoleon said.　As France, so all:
Imagination ruled the world
　Which glittered at the festal ball.
It scarcely saw the smooth-faced boy,
　With soft light hair and sleepy eyes:
It saw Old England's power and joy,
　A great king, in that simple guise.
It looked ahead a few brief years,
　And saw a crown on that young head:
It felt that happiness or tears
　For nations are by monarchs shed.

His Royal Highness led the dance;
　His dress showed less magnificence
Than shoddy coats, whose pride, perchance,
　Grew at his creditors' expense.
He danced like many another there;
　Seemed to admire his partner's eyes;

Touched her small hand, glanced at her hair,
    Indulged in little amorous sighs.
Pardon the mention of this stuff,—
    I write it for your information,
Not to his blame : 'twas well enough,
    And shows man's common conformation.

Gazelle was in Lord Oakland's arms,—
    I hate a waltz worse than the (D)evil,
Unless I'm dancing, which disarms
    My malice and the atrocious evil.
Percy had found a moony miss,
    Rejoicing in a Paris dress,
Just from the States. They hailed in bliss
    The public license for caress.

The elder Earl walked like any king,
    Ruled by imagination too :
He saw what monarchy could bring ;
    He heard the sounding titles ring
On other names, in other times,
    In other halls, in Southern climes.

What kept him from that high estate
    But democratic institutions?
The nation's plebeian estate
    Could but be changed by dissolution.
The Union ! Beggars wed with kings,
    White-handed Luxury with Toil,
Famed Southern chivalry with things
    Fit only to combat the soil !

Sir Henry Lyndon gave his hand,
    Earl clasped it as he were his brother;
His fertile brain had raised his stand
    As high as ever stood another.
"How are American affairs?"
"About to make a culmination;
We have the cravens in our lairs;
    We count on England's approbation."

"England has long been looking out
    For startling change in institution:
Youth rarely knows what its about;
    But ignorance meets retribution.
Nations are but concreted men,
    And suffer much in education;
England will grasp your hand, sir, when
    She shall have seen elucidation
By you, that your own theory
    Of politics has failed to save you:
We pity what we can but blame,
    But drink the cup your folly gave you."

"The coming contest is of race;
    Race is the trump which does the winning:
Nature gave us the highest place,
    And we but take it, without sinning.

"War comes to sap the nation's health;
    To slay her sons, and seize her treasure;
We mourn this loss of life and wealth,
    But take it as our safest measure.

We'll fight, and yield not till the death;
  We'll stake brave hearts in our defences;
And, when the North gets out of breath,
  She must defray the incurred expenses!"

" God speed the right if it abide
  With North or South! I warmly wish that
An iron hand work on your side,
  Not covered by a glove of velvet."
Sir Henry Lyndon walked away:
  Earl watched the mazes of the dances,
Thought of life's evanescent play,
  Its splendid schemes, its flitting chances.

Percy and a dashing captain talked
  Of the ladies with impressment;
The grace with which they talked and walked,
  Hark! was their breath all misspent?

" Waltz dances at the ball to-night;
  I think she can rivalry defy,
With her gilding step and touches light,
  Her swaying form and coaxing eye, —
The solace of bachelors such as I."

" Now keep your heart," the captain said,
  " Till I smoke a good Havana,
And then, with the girl with the shining head,
  I'll dance the Varsovienne."

He floated out with a tarletan cloud,
  With rose-wreaths nestling here and there, —

The prettiest girl in the charming crowd
  Of musk and smiles and pearls and hair,
  And every thing that men call fair.

" Now keep your heart," the captain said,
  " But keep your eyes on Anna,
And yield the palm with a whirling head
  To the gay Varsovienne."

Such fitful music, fairy feet
  Just pausing to entrance the eye,
Then flying off with step so fleet,
  You watch in vain, and only sigh
  That they are gone, and wonder why.

" Now keep your heart," the captain said,
  " For by your play you canna,
Give Waltz for the girl with the shining head,
  Hurrah for Varsovienne ! "

They circled round like tipsy sprites,
  Then poised themselves on tiptoe,
Nodded and bowed till awkward wights
  Wondered what they would next do,
  ·When, lo ! they vanished — all through.

" Where is your heart ? " the captain said,
  " Now, by our flag, you canna,
Give Waltz for the girl with the shining head,
  Hurrah for Varsovienne ! "

The music ceased but to commence again.
  Light feet sped to fill up the vacant floor :

I sought a partner, seeking not in vain,
    And gave my soul to Pleasure's own once more.
Mademoiselle Martin, graceful as a fairy,
    An artist, poet, beauty, danseuse,
A girl you'd fancy, but not think to marry,
    More than a flower rocked by the coaxing breeze,
Danced with me. Oh! it was a dainty pleasure
    When her gloved hand fell lightly on mine own,
Like a stray rose-leaf, fluttering with the measure,
    Not caring where its little weight was thrown.
She talked a little with a sweet French accent,
    Admired the flowers, adored the statuettes,
Fluttered her perfumed fan, discussed the advent
    Of recent dancers, State schemes, and coquettes.
" The Prince is coming, sir! Who is that beauty
    Who has the honor of his Highness' arm?
He must admire her if he does his duty:
    She is magnificent, a living charm!"
It was Gazelle: I met her regal glances,
    And knew they spoke of never-changing love;
But how it hurt me! — just the remote chances
    That some bright bawble might attract her love.
I doubted jealously an angel's love.

The dinner was superb: earth, air, and ocean
    Had sent their choicest products to the board;
The red wine swam with such divine emotion
    As makes a beggar happy as a lord.
It flashed in silver, and each rosy beaker
    Did well its part to make light language flow;
It loosed the tongue of many a trembling speaker,
    And tinted foreheads white as Alpine snow.

The hours flew by like a bewildering vision
    Which pains you by its constant brilliancy;
It might be borne by angels in Elysian,
    But not by mortals on this storm-racked sea:
One hour we laugh, another hour we sigh;
    One hour men all seem sanctified, the next depraved;
One day we live, expectant, next day die,
    And find in heaven that peace we long have craved.

The ball broke up; the guests went each his way,
    Hoarding the splendors for a glowing tale,
To tell when time had turned their bright locks gray,
    And children intrigued for a merry tale.
I was as sad as night. 'Twas like the fall
    Of a cloud city driven by the wind,
Its radiant dwellers gone, and, worst of all,
    A bright star faded out, and I left blind.

I saw Gazelle depart, I heard Lord Oakland
    Plead for the pleasure of an early call,
And she allowed him; and her pretty gloved hand
    Gestured a trifle to him, — that was all.

XIV.

ALONE! how strange the mirror looks to-night!
Flashes of light dash o'er its polished face
From where I know not. Not a real light, —
Something you feel and watch, but cannot trace.
It is a ghostly house; I should not start
To see some dead friend take that vacant chair.
Angels must pity my desponding heart,
So aimless, purposeless, and life to dare.
A flash of light, — I see a bright immortal
With burning eyes look at me in the glass:
He brought heaven's radiance through the pearly portal
Which when they visit us the angels pass.
It is my father. In his right hand grasping
A glittering sword, — the sword he used to bear;
While, on a banner his left hand was clasping,
I read, "A purpose, take it, bravely dare."
The apparition fled. A field of battle
With gory terrors slid into its place;
I saw the dead, I heard the fearful rattle
Steal from torn forms, and leave death in its place.
In the dark foreground lay a fallen hero,
Whose features in the vision took no form,
Only the forehead. There had fallen the death-blow,
And there the red blood trickled bright and warm.
A woman with a lantern wandered, weeping,

From corpse to corpse, turning the ghastly light
On each dead face; then, with a shiver, creeping
To yet another, hoping that the light
Would show the one that she alone was seeking.
She turned her lantern on the bloody head,
She knelt, and hearked, touched him, tried gentle
    speaking;
Then moaned in agony, "Dead! he is dead!"
There came a spirit consolation bringing
To her who wept the fall of manhood's strength.
She soothed her with her low, exquisite singing,
Which broke in accents I could hear at length: —

    "He sleeps in death, but not in vain;
    Let joy disperse thy sobs of pain!
    He was the foremost in the fight,
    Because he loved the unsullied right;
    His virtues are his crown of stars,
    More radiant than your blazing Mars.

"Trustingly yield him to loving immortals:
Life is a true life past death's gloomy portals;
Life is a sanctified, earnest endeavor,
Brightening through all the long days of forever.
Thy fallen hero has had no disaster;
For, oh, the true life lies in the hereafter."

    Then I saw the ghosts of heroes
      Rising from the bloody field,
    Like so many maddened Neros
      Massing in the airy field.

Strong in will and resolution,
    As an hour before in life,
They will strike for retribution;
    They will turn not from the strife.
Some bent o'er their dying brothers,
    Others sped to friends and home;
Spirits gone before met others
    Jubilant that they had come.
All were active, earnest, looking
    For some labor to perform,
Scarcely missing their dead bodies
    In their Union uniform.

Then it faded, and another
    Horror slid into the glass
Far more awful than the other.
    First I thought it was a mass
Of revived Egyptian mummies
    Stripped of all their ancient bands,
And left naked. But the scene lies
    Not in far Egyptian lands.
How they plead for food and raiment;
    Long have plead, been long denied.
" Ha!" their keepers shout, " take payment
    Southern justice shall decide.
You look wondrously like ' niggers'
    You have such a fondness for;
Guess you didn't count the figures
    When you launched upon this war.
Starving will abate your ardor;
    Dust is on your Yankee noses,

Suffering will press you harder ;
   You will grow as meek as Moses.'

Ah! the cruelty was hellish.
   Men who grew in luxury
There ate snakes and toads with relish,
   And enjoyed such misery.
Strong men, who went out with valor
   Fed from sources all divine,
Starved, and died in filth and squalor,
   And were thrown to hungry swine.
" Ruling Powers," I cried, " oh ! tell me,
   What is all this sinning for?"
And the feeble voices answered,
   "We are prisoners of war."

Then I saw a radiant goddess,
   With our own flag in her hand,
Call in accents almost hopeless,
   Till it sounded through the land:
" Rally, Northmen! Are you thinking
   You are Hercules at play
With a serpent? You will slay
   Your own offspring if you wake not!
O Columbia, bring thy men!
   Bring me hearts to do and quake not,
Call thy brave and stalwart men!"

Then I heard a consultation
   Running through the prosperous North,
And a common exclamation,
   " Life is more than money worth."

Bags of gold, and rolls of bank-bills,
  Were the answer to the call.
" Take our gold, hire where your mind wills,
  We can spare no time at all."
Then the mills resumed their business,
  And the factories spun again,
Till the disappointed goddess
  Cried again, " I plead for MEN ! "

Then in every town resounded
  Music rallying martial force,
Till the tread of thousands sounded
  Like a nation on one course.
I sprang up to join the numbers
  Stepping to the bugle's tone ;
Springing thus from dreary slumbers,
  Finding peace and I alone.

XV.

One counts Time's passage, at hotels, by meals;
  And breakfast is my choice. It is enjoyment
To see what truth the morning-time reveals
  In character, carefully to the world bent.
Sleep, dreams, and fancy have unbent the mind
  From many insane follies of the day;
Dress, face, and attitude are unconfined,
  And charming Nature takes her own free way.
We step aside from Fashion's rigid code;
  Wear what we will, and wear it as we will;
Think very little of the Paris mode,
  And laugh as wild as an Italian trill.
Slippers blow out like flower-beds in Spring,
  And snowy petticoats are wondrous bold
With dainty tucks and ruffles (poets sing
  Of what they list, at all times, I am told).

I like to sit and watch the guests come in,
  (I like it better than fresh eggs and coffee,)
From burnished gold down to unvalued tin,
  From modern Socrates to silly Sophia.
I looked for her, last seen amid the throng
  Of guests departing from the brilliant scene,
Like some bright star, too heavenly to belong
  To evanescent glitter, surface sheen.
She came, at length, like bright Aurora's child,
  From Oriental chambers of the sun,

Who, by some magic art, had been beguiled
    To walk with mortals, — she the brightest one.
Her wrapper was a rose-hued tissue cloud,
    Shaped to her slight waist by a sash of white;
Her long, bright hair in rippling wavelets flowed
    Around her figure, as if snaring light;
A burnished star glowed on her waxen breast,
    And in the profuse folds of either sleeve,
Like dainty glories stopping there to rest
    Until the coming of their owner, — Eve.

She saw me, and came to me with a smile:
"Allow me, sir, to breakfast at your side;
Papa is late, — in European style, —
    And Percy went out for an early ride."
I thanked her for the great consideration,
    Ordered her dishes, praised her courteously,
And, with but very little demonstration,
    Was just as happy as a man can be, —
Or nearly so. I incidentally
    Mentioned her promenading with the Prince.
She laughed a little, and said carelessly,
"I have had prettier beaus before, — and since."
"What did he talk of? — pardon me for asking."
    "Ah, yes! He gives one splendid common-places, —
I don't recall one. I'm not fond of tasking
    My mind too much. He praised the flowers and vases,
And our State ladies with divine impressment;
    Their brief, ethereal beauty, brightening
Each generation in a soul-refinement,
    Which is far purer than its fountain spring.

" Papa is rapturous in his praise of many,
   And of Lord Oakland in particular.
Fie on a title! I'd not give a penny
   For names and honors won me from afar.
They nurture indolence, kill self-reliance,
   Make others shapers of our destiny,
Set merit and misfortune at defiance,
   And steal from others what ourselves should be.
I am republican : I am for giving
   Honor to him who earns the laurel wreath ;
Great acts, to count, must be of one's own living ;
   They're nothing if we take them like a thief.
Oh, I am crazed ! the world is such a tumult,
   And black Injustice grasps the throat of Right ;
I sometimes think this strange life is an insult
   Thrust on us by a demon strong in might.
They tell us that the world is growing better,
   And will be trod by angels white as light ;
That God, in his good time, will break the fetter
   That long has clanked upon the feet of Right.
It must be so ; but what a round of ages
   Loom in the future to that blessed time !
A score of centuries hence will the life pages
   Of those who live be scarred as deep as mine."

" But now, Gazelle, a heaven-born sense of justice
   Is something to be hoarded, and not used :
The man who deals in it will find his trust is
   In something for which he will be abused.
He'd be as poor as old Diogenes, —
   A helpless victim to the vulture throng
Who think of Justice less than sleek-faced Ease,
   And of their wants much more than doing wrong.

You — would *you* love me, stripped of every thing
   We call refinement, cultivation, taste?
The high-born Cupid flies on gleaming wing,
   He's over-careful where his hopes are placed.

" He would not wear a pair of cowhide boots,
   Tweed pantaloons, and shilling palm-leaf hat,
If it were one of God's ordained pursuits,
   And he could save the world by doing it.
And you — allow me — would not be the frame
   For such rare drapery and jewels bright,
If wealth were equal. You are not to blame,
   More than the sun is for his golden light.
Equality seems not to be a part
   Of Nature's plan, search for it where you will:
She loves all offspring of her wondrous art, —
   The cold gray mountain and the sunny hill, —
But showers her gifts with most capricious hand:
   One place she makes the valleys glow with flowers,
Another spreads a waste of burning sand;
   Over one land she pours the crystal showers,
And lets another parch: she scatters fruits
   In rare abundance through the blooming South,
But leaves the Northmen such uncouth pursuits
   As spearing seal to fill a hungry mouth.
One bird is brilliant as a flying gem,
   Another dull as a winged bit of earth;
One flower is beauty's essence on its stem,
   Another ugly, and devoid of worth.
She makes some faces lovely, like your own,
   Some charmless as a wooden Hindoo god;
Some voices win us by their silvery tone,
   While others smite us like an iron rod.

In some men's brains, she puts the faculty
    To gather gold, and put it to good uses;
Makes others beggars, heirs to misery,
    Fit subjects for misfortunes cold abuses.
I used to think reforming this great earth
    On every Christian's trembling shoulders lay;
But recently my brain has given birth
    To this: "Let Nature take her own good way."

Observe that sleepy fellow sitting yonder,
    Less than a pygmy, some, in point of size:
He is a wit. Dame Nature made a blunder
    In giving him those sleepy-looking eyes.
He is a sergeant under that young captain;
    Sick of red tape and style, I should presume;
He thinks such dash and frippery is all vain,
    As evanescent as West End perfume.
He eyes disdainfully those pompous Frenchmen
    Talking of horses, women, and so forth,
Like hurried magpies, more than gentlemen,
    And they will get a thrust of sterling worth.
"Be Gad, be Gad!" they ring in every sentence,
    As if it were the brightest thing they know.
Louis Napoleon would make less pretence,
    And fair Eugénie is not more for show.

Bob throws himself back in his roomy chair,
    Stretches his napkin o'er his narrow breast:
"Waitah, come here, sir! don't stand there and stare
    Like a young owl on track of a hen's nest!
Order me span of blacks — I'll take me grays —
    In fifteen minutes — that's a lively lad:

Hold on! Order the thousand-dollar chaise,
   Also me wife, and I'll ride out, be Gad!"

The waiter stares: he knows the wag has got
   Horses nor chaise nor wife, — nothing but wit.
" Increase your movements! Bring them on the
     spot,
   Or with me gaitah you'll get sorely hit!"

The tables roar. The waiter hangs his head;
   The Frenchmen smirk to hide their wounded
     pride;
And Bob walks out with a majestic tread,
   To take a smoke before his splendid ride.

The elder Earl came in, bland as October,
   Fresh from his dreams of lordship and new
     power;
But, when he saw myself, looked wondrous sober,
   And changed from sweet to most decided sour:
He must have read from some unwary glances,
   By intuition, or some careless move,
That not improbably the best of chances
   Were that his daughter and I were in love.
We left the breakfast-room, M. Earle remarking,
   " That Miss Gazelle must keep her time in view,
(I wish, thought I, the old scamp were embarking,)
   And, mind, Lord Oakland is to call at two."

The hours sped on. I saw his grand equipage
   And liveried servant wheel in stately view,
His comely lordship emerge from the carriage
   Imposingly in broadcloth rich and new.

I felt inclined to call him deused ugly,
  And magnify a scholarly stooping;
But I bethought me what a rival should be,
  And sent such evil jealousies a-trooping;
He looked distinguished: attitude and feature
  Spoke unmistakably of noble blood;
Yet if Humility had been his teacher,
  He'd not have borne himself more grandly good.
He wore a look of power and condescension
  Which painters give the faces of our Lord;
No egotism, yet self-comprehension,
  Something which made one hang upon his word.
He tarried long; and, when he took his carriage,
  Looked sad and thoughtful, why I could not guess,
As an old bachelor dreaming of marriage,
  And counting on its bliss or wretchedness.
Gazelle had sung and played with great complete-
    ness;
  Was that the reason he had staid so long?
Or had the fairy Love in tones of sweetness
  Bid him do homage with her dreaming throng?
Oh, love is sweet, and every living creature
  Is titled to the happiness it brings;
Oh, who could close his eyes to that sweet preacher,
  An angel with balm dropping from its wings?

At night he sent a present, — such a present
  As men give women, though they meaning smile,
And say the love of them is time all misspent,
  And they can't sense their fancy for the style.
It was a snowy poodle, small enough
  To have come from the realm of " little folks,"

Or be sent back again by just a puff
   Of breath, or surely on a cloud of smoke.
Its dancing eyes were just a little speck
   Of jet dropped in a shaking rift of snow.
It wore a golden collar on its neck,
   Set thick with sapphires with their azure glow.

A note came with it, begging that Miss Earl
Accept the trifling gift, and call it " Pearl."
He begged a slight remembrance at her hands,
Though his life-lines were thrown in other lands,
And told her that her memory was a pleasure
Which every coming day would bring him pleasure.
He also mentioned a consideration
Of her loved father : 'twas an invitation
To visit, when he would, his own plantation ;
He hoped public affairs might bring him thither,
And begged her that their friendship should not wither
Until they should again clasp hands together.
He spoke of sailing on the coming day,
And hoped her life would be a lengthened May ;
Meanwhile the Great Dispenser of all good
Keeping her soul in its pure angelhood !

Next morning, Percy, whistling " Yankee Doodle,"
Rapped at my door holding the noble poodle,
Saying he came to win congratulation
On this arrival. Our association
With this embassy of a foreign nation
Called for, he thought, a dash of demonstration.

He said Gazelle had boxed his ears right soundly,
And his good father had reproved him roundly ;

Therefore he plead for pity most profoundly.
He said Gazelle (blessings upon the lady!)
Used it as tenderly as 'twere a baby,
And asked me if I thought that costly thing
Was the forerunner of a wedding-ring, —
Meaning the collar. Pearl peered up his eyes,
And eyed us both in innocent surprise.

Oh! by the way, he asked when are we going
To the White Mountains. Autumn winds are blowing,
And, ere we wist, old Winter will be snowing
On those bleak tops. 'Tis time that we were going.

My father starts for home early to-morrow,
(I shall not think of that, thought I, with sorrow ;)
This is a sudden change, but seems essential
To some large matters of the Presidential
Election. It is very consequential
That our affairs shape in a proper way,
And that we see to it, and have fair play.

If that rail-splitter Lincoln is elected,
Some Southern cannonading is expected,
And some secession ways may be detected
Which loyal Yankees will desire corrected;
But, if their basis come to be inspected,
It will be found the whole heart is affected.

But let affairs of State pursue their course,
And Southern steel combat with Northern force;
We will be friends through all the mazy years
Allotted us, though fraught with joys or tears.

Give me your hand, and pledge me I shall be,
Living or dead, shrined in your memory:
I have a nameless dread of fading out
From my friends' hearts, since living there will be,
As I decipher Nature's lessons out,
My only claim to immortality.

Nature hoards not her rude, imperfect types,
But yields them one by one to sure decay;
And in her time gloomy Oblivion wipes
Each vestige of their transient life away.
Continents change; islands rise up and flee;
The mighty oceans leave their oozy beds;
Plants, animals, and man change constantly;
And new life on the corpse of lower treads:
Race after race has lived and toiled and gone;
Their names, existence, habits, known to none.
When, lo! when fifty thousand years have fled,
A new race finds entombed these ancient dead
In the earth's strata, and their history
Earth yields at last, though steeped in mystery.
This is the tale of science differing
Widely from what is called an offering
From an all-wise and justice-loving God
To man, — the Bible. Has he also trod
The ways of progress? Verily this looks
As if he speaks in works not as in books.

  I cannot see what strange economy
   Of God hoards up human intelligence,
  Called human souls, through all eternity,
   Though they be ignorance and sin intense.

" And can you see economy, my friend,
    If this stupendous thing the universe,
With all its mighty workings, has no end
    But to build up, and ruthlessly destroy?
An untaught fool, a wanton, trifling boy,
    By no bad accident could plan a worse.
Through all God's works, I see a vasty plan
    Which ultimates in immortality:
On the vast pyramid of life stands man, —
    Life which has wrought his higher destiny.

" And you will wake from all these hateful dreams
    In a new land of sweet realities;
And I shall see you in those sinless years
    Enjoying what you fancied could not be,
When your dark eyes gazed through mortality."

XVI.

A MELLOW August morning woke from sleep
   A tired fellow, whose whole comprehension
Centred in gratitude profound and deep
   Upon the framer of that great invention;
But looking from my window in the glen,
   Where I had come, I scarce remember when,
I gazed on Nature's most bombastic freaks,—
   The towering heights of the White-Mountain peaks.

The sun climbed slowly up through fog and cloud,
   And filled the emerald valley full of light;
Its silver waves flashed o'er the mountains proud.
   The children of such unimagined night,
Clay, Adams, Jefferson, colossal stand
   With Washington. What grandeur they dispense
By their proud names! Forever more will stand
   The intellects and their grand monuments.

The evanescent clouds in fields of air
   Play lightly round those everlasting peaks,
Hanging their drapery and shadows there,
   Then flying off with morning's rosy streaks
Glowing among their folds. The evergreens
   On Carter's summit talk in lights and shades
Of their enjoyment of the aerial scenes
   Which flit in loveliness above their heads.

I always had a love for mountain heights
  As pictured in the distance. I suppose,
When one eyes closely all their minute sights,
  The rugged and unlovely they disclose.
But yet I longed to tread those cloudy peaks,
  And pierce their far-off hidden mysteries;
Stand where the wind in its wild accents speaks,
  And the hoar Frost-King's constant dwelling is.
The superstitious Indian shrunk in dread
  From treading higher than the flowers and moss:
Manito dwelt there, and would fiercely shed
  His wrath on him who dared their tops to cross.
But the Caucasian with his glowing face
  And lantern brain has searched each shadowy place,
Sent his red brother to a new abode,
And driven with him his mysterious God.
The lightnings playing in the summer skies
Are not the flashing of his wrathful eyes;
The gorgeous clouds, trimmed by the setting sun,
Are not the robes the red man's God has on.

Where are we going? What will people say
  Of things which we call godly mysteries,
When Science lights her torches all the way?
  Our dreams now point to great realities.
There will be nothing supernatural,
  But all things bow to some eternal law,
With matter co-existent. The great all
  Of miracle will be a man of straw.
Don't shut this book, and burn it at the stake,
  But have a little patience. Bear in mind

I may be wrong, or you in a mistake;
    So treat me and my hair-brained offspring kind.
Bear this: I should not be the first to err,
    Nor you the first to feel intolerant;
And, if your righteous judgment you defer,
    I shall appreciate the compliment.

Premising it is I and a few others
    Who do the drama of the famed ascension,
Which would so terrify a loving mother
    She'd choose more ignorance and less pretension,
We took an early breakfast, and set out
    In splendid spirits, in a crazy stage,
With only dreams of what we were about;
    And for adventure in a mortal rage.
We were to tread the cloud-capped mountain height
    Which pierced the azure of the Southern sky,
Talk with the wind, look down on landscapes bright,
    And suffer every thing, — except to die.

The old stage bumped, not rocked, — it had no springs, —
    Which made us laugh; then all began to talk:
I told Gazelle she ought to use her wings;
    A homely spinster said she "orter walk."
The ladies grew a little confidential,
    Observed the country was fearfully stony:
'Twould be precarious to get a fall
    E'en from the back of a dwarf Indian pony.

"Ho!" said the driver. "Out, select your horses
    And saddles for a long and tumbling ride."

I hope when Common Sense marshals her forces,
   And simpering Folly shall have run her courses,
She'll tell the ladies they may ride astride!

Poor things! They put on skirts as long as baby's,
   And then were mounted like such helpless things
As infants, riding off like giant May-bees,
   (We'll get there!) with enormous cotton wings.
I do presume that any common *man*
   Rigged in like way, and made to ride a horse
Up Washington after the female plan,
   Would be brought down a bruised and mangled corpse.

Slowly the mist crept up the mountain steep,
   And floated off, not like the evening dew,
But like a snowy flock of lazy sheep
   Roaming the meadows of empyrean blue.
Soft foliage hung above dark mossy rocks;
   Bright berries glistened in the rising 'sun;
And laughing little girls in rustic frocks,
   With busy fingers, picked them one by one.
We caught the gleam of waters now and then
   Dashed in a landscape dropped between the hills,
Or a white farm-house in a distant glen,
   And barns and orchards, and gay thread-like rills.

The spectral forest, looking like a freak
   Of crazy genii, rose upon our sight:
I harked to hear some stalking goblin speak,
   And say our bones would some day bleach as white.

O marble trees! you stretch your naked limbs
    And your dead roots in vain for Summer's wreath:
She tells you that old age is full of whims,
    And you should long ago have lain beneath
The soil on which your outer garb was cast.
Your life and use and beauty all are past:
Moveless and dumb you meet the wintry blast,
And shiver not; gleam in the summer sun,
And feel no life. The changing seasons run
Their Heaven-appointed courses annually,
Changing all else, but not affecting thee.

A cataract of cloud came sweeping down
Upon the dead white trees, clothing their limbs
In its gray drapery, as if it longed
To beautify what had been deeply wronged
By some arch enemy. It caught upon the twigs,
And made them look like little living sprigs
Of smoke-tree. But too soon the unpitying wind
Tore it away, and sent it on to find
A parching valley, which was growing brown
In August sunshine. Scantly Summer trims
The Mount in green as we ride slowly higher
Over the crooked pathway up this granite spire.

The bushes stop, but feathery ferns climb on,
    And o'er rough rocks the pretty lichen creeps:
Then, ere we wist, the waning ferns are gone,
    And the white Alpine flower its summer keeps
In spreading out a little flowering star,
Which looks as if it wandered from afar,
And paled and languished for a warmer home:
But the winds scolded it, and told of none.

The ponies, slow and careful, climbed the path,
    Leaping steep passes, treading rolling rocks,
Broken as if a giant in his wrath
    Had knocked in pieces some gigantic blocks :
It was as rugged as the steeps of life,
    But wearied us for only a brief day ;
While this great other holds us to the strife
    While weary years crawl like dull snails away.
I often wish that I could dash it off
    With one mad effort, since I cannot pass it ;
For all our goodness meets with demon scoff.
    If I could have my choice, oh, I would pass it !
Dreams — what are they ? Playthings our nurse
        Fate gives us,
    Which make our silly souls grow wild with joy.
Ah, how we mourn when Destiny o'ertakes us,
    And dashes in our face each treasured toy !
O Destiny ! why not blot out their traces,
    And leave the soul content in poverty ?
You lead us gypsying o'er desert places,
    And Memory holds up pictures which we see,
    And long have sought to find reality.

There where that granite pile stands by the way,
    Topped by a block of quartz of snowy white,
A youthful pilgrim on earth went astray,
    And wandered to the gates of endless light.
She was a guarded blossom, frail and pure
    As a syringa ; and this chilling top
Was more than her sweet frailty could endure :
    And so her soul bade her weak body stop,
And it went home, leaving its twin-born mate
    In the damp fog so dense, that e'en the love

Of two fond parents pierced its folds too late
  To hold their darling from her home above.
Oh! fearful must have been the agony
  Of their bowed hearts to hear the failing tone,
The lengthening breath, and strain their eyes to see.
  But could not, — silence told them she had gone
In to the sunlight of the great Unknown;
  And they two suffered and endured alone.

A sigh for Lizzie Bowen. Time will fling
Her memory onward as a mournful thing
For travellers to handle as they ride
By the rough grave-stone on the mountain-side
Which marks the rugged spot on which she died.

A little farther up, and I will shout
Until the mountains wonder who is out,
And, more especially, what he's about.

The ladies were alive, and yet could speak,
  Which last they did deprecatingly,
Of mountain travelling. They were less weak
  In admiration than in strength to see.
They like adventure in sugar-pill doses
  (The undiluted tincture is too strong,
And this was tincture): they nigh froze their noses
  A sultry August day, and screamed so long
From very fright, that their sweet voices sounded
  Like a learned parrot's with the whooping-cough.
If you have been there, you know, where you grounded,
  Your whole corporeal body was a laugh.

One thing annoyed you in your hour of pleasure;
  And that was the idea of going down.
You longed to seize some mythologic measure,
  Like gods and genii of ancient renown.
It did not seem improbable you might,
  Since your surroundings were so very strange:
You were above earth, clouds, in heaven's plain sight,
  For supernatural views in splendid range.

No eye for scenery now, we shiver so!
  The winds are merciless and wintry cold;
They laugh, and say, " You little things should know
  That you are sensitive, and we are bold."
" Tip-top House," and a wreath of curling smoke
  Issuing from its chimney, was a sight,
Which, more than scenery which in grandeur broke
  Below us, filled me with a sane delight.
How willingly I handed out a " quarter"
  To warm my stiffened fingers by a fire,
And a new sixpence for a drink of water!
  I never sensed before the worth of fire.

A dinner of beefsteak swimming in butter,
  And boiling coffee, and such cheering things,
Thawed me sufficiently, so I could utter
  The transports which the view of grandeur brings.

Poets sing overmuch of mountain splendors.
  " Why?" (I will tell you, friend:) they never travel,
Else they would sooner praise an Irish bender
  Than sing of ugly rocks and heaps of gravel.

But I am on the summit. I have earned
    The beauty I enjoy ; and, what is more,
Gazelle is with me, and you must have learned
    That Love adds pinions, if the soul will soar,
And with a soft and iridescent light
    Bathes meanest objects with a heavenly hue,
The brain bewilders, and the enraptured sight
    Sees castles glittering in the vacant blue.

The thin cold air enchanted, or else Love :
    The fact is, I did feel somewhat uncommon.
There was but little one could see above,
    Below ; but of it let the poets hum on.
We had a poet with us. He was one
    Just starting out to travel with his Muse :
Scaling the mountains was tremendous fun ;
    No pain to him was cold or slip or bruise :
With us upon the largest rock he stood,
    The keen wind blowing out his lengthy hair ;
He wished another mountain rose, he would
    Climb higher yet, and drink the enchanting air.

"Look off," said he : " what splendors spread below !
    The earth has heaved these billows in her wrath,
Backed by the fires which in her centre glow
    Far, far below the storm-wind's rocky path."

Yonder the sea, — a line of silver tends
    Almost a hundred miles away, 'tis said :
There Saco like a dream of beauty wends ;
    Northward Katahdin rears his dreary head ;
Across this gulf a line of peaks arise, —

Clay, Adams, Jefferson, and Lafayette, —
Names which America cannot forget ;
And, see ! among the hills the azure skies
Reflected by a lake, — the Lake of Clouds.
How gorgeous is the light which bathes them
 all !
A dreary mist the farthest distance shrouds,
And purple vestures o'er the nearer fall.
The rocks are dyed in beauty ; and the heart
Beats in the measure of seraphic songs,
Praising the master of such wondrous art
Which only to Omnipotence belongs.

Below us rush the tempests, and the world
Feels the warm pelting of the summer rain :
We are above ; we see the clouds unfurled,
And lurid lightnings pierce their aqueous veins ;
But, grander yet, above, the clear bright sun
Shines undisturbed upon the surging mass :
Unmoved he rides the ages slowly on,
While men and nations swift to chaos pass.

I wish I had a boat, I'd launch it now, —
'Twould float off finely from this mountain's brow !

That lightning plays swift as a serpent's tongue
The caverns of the thunder-caps among.
Oh, blinding splendors from the tempest wrung !
My ecstasy scorns wildly my control :
I feel the Infinite break on my soul ;
And I feel truly that I am a son
Of Him who drives the cosmic chariot on.

" My friend," I said, " I have been entertained
By your expression of these granite heights ;
But people sometimes get a bit hair-brained
By coming where the air is pure and light.
I wish you had that boat, I'd help you launch ;
Undoubtedly you'd think it more than nice.
But much I fear your courage, fierce and stanch,
Would soon give out, and have me hung for
    vice.

" I wish you great good luck, sir, in your goings,
    Though they be round the wonder-freighted
        earth ;
But my opinion is, a few such blowings
    Would send your spirit through a second birth."

He heard me not. His face turned up, imploring
Some airy sprite, where his great soul was soar-
    ing,
Perhaps the weather-clerk, to send more sunshine,
And let him deeper drink of beauty divine.

We left the little house, which seemed so much
    Like a big play-house piled up in a day,
Of small rough stones. A well-directed touch
    Of comfort, in her unassuming way,
Had hung up cotton-prints o'er the rough wall
    So plebeian like, but soft and warm withal,
It seemed to one to be the very thing
    Most wanted there. The patient ponies bring
Upon their backs, up the long tiresome way,
    From the green valley, wood and food each day.

Down the rough bridle-path, telling each other
    Our own opinion of Mount Washington;
And far too tired to think much of another
    Ascent: reached home at ten, the drama done.

XVII.

An hour for a parting, a moment for tears!
Oh! life is so subtle, and changeful its years,
The things that we prize most, and claim as our own,
Slip out of our grasp, and like sunshine have flown.
An hour for a parting! Oh! do not disguise
The sharp shafts of sorrow, but look in my eyes;
For days may be coming when sadness and night
Will darkle where now is love's tremulous light.

An hour for a parting! Oh! utter some word
Which over life's tumult will ever be heard
Like music which sounds o'er the tramping of feet
Which press on to battle. The moments are fleet:
I eagerly hearken to hear what you say, —
Be kind, now; remember I'm going away.
I have kissed you, you know, in the days that are
    gone;
Let me kiss you to-night by the bliss we have known.
Let me kiss you: you cannot say *no* in your heart,
When so long we must wander so lonely apart:
I know you will think of me, and it shall be
As one who would honor you now constantly,
And throw not a shade on a pure memory.
But, ah! you are dear to me, dearer than life;
So dear, you will bless me by being my wife,
If Fate dashes not the sweet cup from my lips,
And throws not o'er happiness gloom and eclipse.

The future is shadow, but now you are mine, —
Your sweet winning answers and beauty divine.
Oh! lay your light hand, while you may, in my own:
I shall bless you and think of it when I am gone.
Oh! tell me you feel we shall meet when the storm
Shall have passed, and the skies are unclouded and warm!
Will you clasp this same hand — give me truly your word —
If from pressing your own it next presses a sword?
I loathe the dread carnage, the spilling of blood;
But I loathe the foul cesspool where freedom has stood:
And, if I should die, why, the motive is not
How long one can live, but how much one can do.
If to do much and die early should be my lot,
I should not regret it, but joyous renew,
Existence and effort in that glowing clime
Which lies through a cypress-wreathed gateway of Time.
You know what is coming; you know the wild Night
Will descend in her sables, her mourning and woe;
And a nation, grown up in prosperity's light,
The fathomless depths of misfortunes will know;
And thousands will weep o'er their dear fallen braves
Who march off to music in martial array,
But never march back, for the doors of the grave
Will close on their goings forever. Away
With such tear-laden thoughts! you are bowing your head
Like a white flower whose chalice is heavy with dew.
Look up; do not weep until sorrow is shed
On your head, and black clouds shut away heaven's blue.

An hour for a parting! The hour has been mine,
And far in the future its moments will shine.
When next we shall meet, we may be something
    changed ;
But pledge me, Gazelle, we shall not be estranged :
That thought will be dearer than aught you could give,
And something well worth a great longing to live.
And so the girl pledged me, and rained her hot tears
On my hand she was wringing in passionate grief,
Half-whispering hopes, and half-murmuring fears,
And praying the dread separation be brief.

And after a moment I found myself going
Along a hard pavement, where ; I hardly knowing.

XVIII.

UNCLE SAMUEL's boys are dashing:
  They have answered to his call
To assist at his great threshing, —
  Stout and slender, short and tall.
Country pumpkins, city gentry,
  Every thing but dapper dandies:
They are where they always will be, —
  Sporting styles, and giving candies.

O'er the fields, like Shanghai hencoops,
  Stand the tents so white and new;
The parade-ground of the new troops
  Glitters with its gold and blue.
Flags, resplendent in their glory,
  Float above the earnest heads,
Without bullet-holes and story,
  Honors gory battle sheds.

Officers from many sources,
  With new swords and heavy plumes,
Drill as best they can their forces,
  Innocent of powder-fumes;
Straight as candles they go marching
  Back and forth, and shifting arms;
Over straight, so they are arching,
  Ears pricked up at sham alarms.

Out on guard and picket-duty,
  Mud above their tall boot leather;
Firm in thinking that a beauty
  Lies in disciplining, whether
Danger lurks a thousand miles off,
  Or a league outside the camp.
As it was the former, why scoff
  At the power which made them tramp?

Pardon me for merry-making
  Over matter grave as this:
Those first volunteers were taking
  Lessons which came not amiss.
This was mimicry: the real
  More imposingly begun
Than the play of the ideal
  In the battle of Bull Run.

Letters went to many a household
  After that disastrous day,
Freighted with a bloody tale, told
  In a soldier's simple way:
How they fought their first great battle,
  How they saw a comrade fall,
How a shell burst, how the rattle
  Of balls scared them — not at all.

But to many a home made lonely
  Went no letter, nor a word;
But the printed dead-list only,
  Which confirmed what they inferred.

Then we learned the war meant something
　More than a capricious freak ;
That not strength nor skill was wanting
　On the side we deemed so weak.

Then we learned a swart-faced giant,
　With his million bloody hands,
In an attitude defiant
　On our nation's vitals stands ;
Then began the fearful crying
　Of unnumbered shattered hearts,
Which in time sinks into sighing,
　That remains till life departs.

XIX.

"Halt!" came down the lines. We were planted to
    the soil;
Our feet were tired of marching, and we gladly ceased
    from toil.
I looked all ways around me: far as the eye could see
Surged the tidal human ocean, gleamed war's gorgeous
    panoply.
The glittering of bayonets, the beautiful blue mail,
The gallant flag we fought for, floated out against the
    sky,
Like the drapery of freedom, guarding us with jealous
    eye;
At the peril of her honor would an army dare to die!
There was silence in the ranks; but afar upon the
    gale
Came the neighing of the war-horse, and the officers'
    commands;
Or, in other words, the great brain speaking to the
    willing hands.
The jar of the artillery awoke a distant rumbling,
Which came down upon the winds like an earthquake's
    sullen grumbling.

We could not see our foemen. Nature was at spring-
    time rest,
Dreaming to the singing streamlets, with her blossoms
    on her breast:

Her living spires of emerald stood thick beneath our feet,
And the trees with bloom were redolent, the air was moist and sweet,
The verdant hills swelled round us like fixed concreted waves;
Ah, we knew full well their bosoms would be our slain ones' graves!
But we did not stop to wonder which of us would moulder there;
We only clasped our rifles, and swore to do and dare.

Off where the foe was hidden in the forest's darkling shade,
The glances of the soldiers like angry meteors played,
Till they heard the cannon's booming; and the clouds of rolling smoke
Were hung up before the forest like a monstrous sable cloak,
From behind which came the enemy, and wound around our force
Like a slowly moving milleped who knew his proper course.
Our Scandinavian hero gave his orders, well defined,
And they came on flying chargers, who had left the winds behind:
"Advance! For Minie-balls give Minies, for grape return them grape:
So continue. Fight like Greeks, my boys, and keep in compact shape."

A herd of yelling bipeds was unleashed against us then ;
Foul hell's prospective prodigies, but now barbarous men,—
Chocktaw, Chicksaw, and Cherokee,— names that the Devil loves,
Because they do his coarsest work without the aid of gloves ;
Not enough their fiendish cruelty, the Southrons gave it aid
In the way of drugged " fire-water." It was just they were betrayed ;
And the draught they had concocted for us, they too had to drink :
That was a phase of warfare of which they did not think.
Their war-whoops scared the wild birds from their warbles in the wood,
But they daunted not our soldiery ; like iron men they stood,
While they listened in amazement. Then came the whiz of balls
Like a hail-storm which in summer on a growing harvest falls ;
And beneath the angry pelting many a high heart ceased to beat,
While to the land of shadows their spirits beat retreat.
" Target-practice ! " said the chieftains, and no sooner was it said
Than we faintly saw the red men dropping on a gory bed,
As a surgeon would have told us, from an overdose of lead.

They grew maddened at the carnage in their covert
   in the woods;
They had wanted less assistance in their work of shed-
   ding blood;
They rushed out with the scalping-knife among our
   wounded men,
And to those who lay a-dying did death's cruel work
   again.
They were worse than human beings. They were
   demons in a high rage,
And the innate hate they bore us slaked itself in
   reckless carnage.
The glowing sun descended on a storm-tossed airy sea,
And the stars amid the tempest gleamed red and
   fearfully.
We were worn with heavy fighting, we had been so
   hotly pressed;
So, forgetting the to-morrow, on the field we sank to
   rest.

The east blazed into scarlet at the rising of the sun,
Then again the fell destruction with all vigor was
   begun;
But his setting beams fell on us without the battle
   won.
The third day, still resisting, looking like men made
   of smoke,
Set on fire, we sensed the burden, and that heavy was
   the yoke.
Brave Siegel called upon his men to rally once again,
And told them, by the dear old flag, it should not be
   in vain.

Then the cannon belched its thunder till the earth
    shook 'neath the sound,
And mortal forms like autumn leaves were rifted on
    the ground.
Well aimed, the heated cannon sent their sulphureous
    breath
On with the iron missiles, all messengers of death :
Their booming shook the heavens; then came the
    order, " Charge ! "
The men rushed to the onslaught with flashing steel
    in air,
And souls which cared not if an hour found them
    disrobed and bare.
So victory came with the change which now is known
    as death ;
But which, in truth, is breathing deep of God's reviving
    breath.
The foe fled, panic-stricken ; crazy cavalry pursued
Till there was no further danger that the fighting be
    renewed.
Oh, wild the exultation when we saw the army yield !
And the field was ours ! ours victory ! but, oh ! the
    field, *our field !*
The grass was trodden in the dust, now emerald no
    more ;
And the rootlets of its trampled blades had drunk their
    fill of gore :
The battle-smoke rose sullenly into the twilight skies,
And the stars looked through it like a veil thrown
    over Beauty's eye.
The moon like some young angel, as pitying and calm,
Looked from the clouds, and on each beam dropped
    off a little balm.

Oh, it was blessed! just the sight of her, so white and
still,
To us, who from the early dawn had worked to crush
and kill.
I wandered restlessly abroad now the dread day was
done,
The fighting through, our foemen fled, a brilliant con-
quest won.
The evening air, sulphureous, bore to my deadened
ears
The moans and groans and anguish-sobs which utter
more than tears.
It is not overhard to die, shot in the battle's din ;
But to be torn and wrecked, and still have life remain
within
A body blown a dozen ways, holding to life for
days,
Without a hope of life on earth beyond those torturing days,
Bearing each hour a thousand deaths, is overmuch to
die ;
But we must take things as they come, and not be
asking why.

When the fighting raged the hottest in the early of
the day,
I had seen her lordly father — Gazelle's — in war's
array :
He took a brigade forward, and, amidst the rain of
ball,
Kept them so firm, you would have said, " They care
not if they fall."

A jetty charger, glittering like midnight with her
    stars,
Arched his lithe neck, as proud to bear an officer with
    bars
Upon his shoulder-straps, which told he was a rebel
    captain,
An aide to the old general, his father. Oh the sharp
    pain
Which pierced me when I knew my hand was raised
    against her brother,
And one I loved! but soldiers learn the soul and
    heart to smother.
He scarcely seemed to me a friend, but some star tragic
    actor
Upon an unknown stage, — a man with the strong arm
    of Hector,
And as sad fate, perchance. Who says death and the
    brave keep strangers?
It is not so. He stays from death who stays most
    out of dangers.
I came to where the fearful charge had been made
    and repulsed:
Death held his victims in all ways; some placid, some
    convulsed,
Frozen to stillness when their cause needed their
    efforts most.
Oh! then I sensed most fearfully what victory had
    cost,
And that, though we had richly gained, God's other
    side had lost;
For we are all his children, doing each the best he can,
Working out his own appointment, high or low, in one
    great plan.

The furious cavalry had swept over the bloody
place,
And iron hoof-prints might be seen on many a ghastly
face
And broken skull, as on they rushed to crush a flying
foe :
Then followed the artillery, drawn by its score of
horses,
Rolling its ponderous wheels upon the groaning men
and corses,
Ending many a lengthened pang by one resistless
blow.
That avalanche of ruin passed, and some were living
yet,
Moaning alone, slashed by the sword or pierced by
bayonet;
While now and then a muttered curse, pressed from
the soul by pain,
Fell on the deaf unlistening ears of those more kindly
slain.
It was a fearful sight to see the intellect and
power
Which leaped in vigor in the morn, dead in the evening hour!
A dread foreboding seized my heart; I felt as if a
ghost —
A presence I had some time known — threw a thin
shade acrost
My pathway; but I hurried on; I saw a light
ahead, —
A lantern, in the hands of one robbing the helpless
dead.

"Bring hither!" hither with the light a half-revealing
  beam
Fell on a soldier at my feet, flashing a ghostly
  gleam
Upon a marble face, which smiled a grim determined
  smile,
As he had wearied, and lain down to rest a little
  while.
I sank upon his bosom; oh! was this the mournful
  end
Of Percy, — him I loved so well, — her brother and
  my friend?
Rigid and cold and mute he lay. One scarcely could
  tell why,
But for a little crimson spot upon his forehead
  high.
Death entered there! "Percy," I cried, "O Percy,
  speak to me!
Do you not know that I am here, calling, oh, bit-
  terly?"
Alas! no more those lips will part, no more those
  vacant eyes
Will warm me with their genial glow, warm as the
  May-day skies.
"No more, no more!" I felt those words in their
  most fearful power;
I cursed the laws which made me feel more than the
  tree or flower;
Which gave to man undying loves, far-reaching hopes
  and strange,
And thrust him helpless in a world fraught every hour
  with change.

I felt my utter impotence. I spoke not, thought not, yet
The much I suffered, mute and dumb, I never shall forget:
I writhed in the strong arms of law, immutable as God,
And knew I could not help myself more than a senseless clod.
Then raised the soul its questionings, proportional to its faith:
I doubted justice. How I prayed that I might see his wraith,
If he yet lived, above the wreck of beauteous life and strength!
If he yet lived! *Then* this would be all recompensed at length.
I turned to look upon his horse, still floundering in death,
When something standing at his head made me draw in my breath:
It was a wraith, — it was my friend: he stroked its jetty mane,
And seemed to love and pity it, and try to stop its pain.
He walked to me, and reached his hand, then pointed a thin finger
Far o'er the field, to where a light unmoving seemed to linger:
" Go there," he said, " and tell that one, above one fallen weeping,
That you have seen me, but my form will rise no more from sleeping."

I hastened through the ghostly night to where the
    lonely light
Swung in the hand of one as sad and pitying as the
    night:
"What seek you, lady, here alone? Are any dear to
    you
Who fell upon this fearful day? If so, God strengthen
    you!"
"A brother who rode out at morn with hope in his
    brave breast,
And came not back,—I seek for him: is he among
    the rest?"
"He went down in the fearful charge of crazy man
    and horse,
And I, who loved him, like yourself, have wept above
    his corse.
I wish I need not tell you this; I wish it were not
    true:
Alas for Fate! alas for you! God knows I pity you!"
She turned away, and wrung her hands in speechless
    agony,
Then pleaded in a broken tone, "Oh, show me where
    is he!"

Oh woman's tears! How great the power those
    crystal drops contain!
But o'er the hero at our feet they fell all, all in vain:
They could not melt the grasp of death, and waken
    him again;
But there he slept, whose glossy head was stroked by
    opulence
From boyhood up. Oh, evenly War's blushing hands
    dispense

Her honors! just as soft for him was that damp bed
 of turf
As for the ones who fell with him, though of a lowlier
 birth.
The moon gleamed bright; a sullen dog growled, as,
 with cat-like tread,
The pillagers came up to take the spoils from off *his*
 dead.
His eyes were fire: he louder growled, and shook his
 jetty hair,
And told them in decided terms they could have
 nothing there.
They sneaked away, — for sin is weak, — and the
 brave advocate
Of right laid down again to guard his master, and to
 wait
For his awaking, when a word would make him leap
 with joy,
And his gay whistle and caress the weary watch de-
 stroy.

The aspect of the battle-field is like the desolation
Which a tornado leaves, except its play-ground is the
 nation:

Some killed by shot, shattered by shell, or gashed by
 bayonet;
Some lying in a pool of blood, dying, but living yet;
Some battered by the iron hoofs where swept a thousand horse,
So beaten one could scarcely say the ruin was a
 corpse;

Some perished by the cranching wheels of the artillery;
But some were spared to view the scene, and note the misery.

She passed a door; the bugle call rang on the sullen air.
I would have given wealth or life for that sweet girl's despair;
It hung so cruelly upon a spirit pure as heaven.
But would we bear each other's woes, the power is never given.

XX.

WE woke the sun this morning,
  Preparing extra rations
To last us on our weary march
  To military stations.

The teamsters sung like cherubs
  While tackling their mule-teams,
Their eyes and hair and very hearts
  Snaring the golden sunbeams.

There is so much uncertainty
  In war and its poor chances,
That Hope, the soldier's comforter,
  Says changes are advances.

Hark! hear the song which one glad heart
  Is on the fresh air flinging!
It pleases, innocent of art
  In poetry or singing: —

" The sun was shining brightly one spring day of the
    year,
When my friends and relations began to shed a tear:
I told 'em just to ' simmer down,' there was no use in
    blinkin';
For I was going to Dixie to drive a team for ' Linkin.'

Oh, my! I wish you'd seen me travel,
Going down the turnpike in a cloud of gravel.

" My father said he wanted me to help about his work,
And not rig up in uniform as an excuse to shirk.
I told him it was not my fault my uniform was dashing,
And I was bound to be a hand at Uncle Sam's great thrashing.
Oh, my! you should have seen me going
Down the dusty turnpike puffing and a-blowing.

" When we are old, this war will cause a deal of telling stories,
And we who see the matter through shall wear a weight of glories.
We shall not tell our grandchildren who ask us all about it,
' Darling, ye'r grandpa staid tu hum; did nothing 'tall about it!'
Oh, my! they'll see the mules a-racking
Which grandpa drove in time of war, and hear his whip a-cracking.

" I'm not a broadcloth gentleman, nor officer in tape;
But I can rig a team of mules in decent kind of shape;
And, fifty years from this spring morn, I'll tell my merry stories,
When brigadiers will wear their hats stuck full of gorgeous glories.
Heigh-ho! my Betsy Ann and Nancy;
Set up your ears and arch your necks, and start off kind of fancy."

XXI.

Tented beneath warm Southern skies,
    With foliage sighing overhead,
The golden queen, with languid eyes,
    Her peace and quiet o'er us shed.
We found too many hours for dreams
    About forsaken luxury;
Too many watch-fires sent up gleams
    To the far shores of Memory.

And often in the breathless nights,
    Beneath those Southern skies,
My soul went back to old delights;
    And with uncounted sighs
I thought of *her* whose love and life
    Were all the world to me,
And thanked God for the trifle, life,
    And my idolatry.

I wearied of those days for rest,
    My spirit beat its bars:
I liked the telling fights the best,
    Though won by blood and scars.
The birds, which daily sung among
    The emerald-crested trees,
Seemed but a silly, idling throng,
    Lacking the power to please.

One wearies of the pageantry
  Which decks the ranks of war;
The country's ensigns floating free,
  The glittering leaf and star.
One wearies; for too many times
  Some melting scene of home
Floats through the skies of stranger climes
  When tired feet weariest roam.

It is a dead, external life,
  With all its mighty aims,
Waging a never-ending strife
  Against the spirit's claims;
And, though it ends in mighty good
  To nations, those who fight
To strengthen right by shedding blood
  Endure a milder blight.

But let it go: such things must be,
  And in the glorious end
An individual destiny
  Will find no mourning friend:
However darkly it went down
  To meet its clouded fate,
'Twill glitter nameless in the crown
  Which decks the brow of State.

XXII.

How varied was our work and course
    Would weary you to know :
Sometimes the cannon, booming hoarse,
    Laid ranks of foemen low ;
Now martial music fired the heart,
    And countless colors waved,
While War took on the gorgeous art
    The taste of Mars had craved.

Sometimes, as wild and fierce dragoons,
    We dashed among the trees,
Making the bushes sing us tunes,
    And flutter little glees.
We crushed the flowers to dust again,
    And leaped the daddock pile,
And hunted, with a careless rein,
    The foe in savage style.

Again we made a wicked raid
    Upon some quiet farm,
Frustrating plans carefully laid,
    Without the least alarm.
We took the honey from the hives,
    And milked the willing cows ;
We robbed the chickens of their lives,
    And paid in *script* and bows.

Nothing seemed strange or out place
  For gentleman or clown;
Few tricks were looked on with disgrace,
  But covered with renown.
We came to wear War's heavy yoke,
  Stuck full of common posies
Of thistles, dandelions, and poke,
  Because we found no roses.

XXIII.

HANGING A SPY.

THE sharp air is icy with dribbling sleet;
The hard ground is snow-covered under our feet:
Nature seems to have dressed herself fitly to meet
The cold-hearted multitude thronging the street.
It is strange, it is strange, that men's eyes hunger so
For the sights which reveal but an agonized woe.
How eager they watch! how they bend to each throe
Till the whole heart is sick, and the blood will not flow!
When, but for their eyesight, they never would know
Of the fathomless depths of humanity's woe.

" What is it," you ask me, " that surges the crowd?"
A man on a coffin! a form for a shroud!
A poor, doomed immortal is sentenced by men
To go from the earth to his Maker again.
Man is so short-sighted! O God, is it just,
When he says to that throbbing heart, " Turn back to the dust"?
Thou wast its Creator, and thine is the trust.

But hark! the sad music creeps out on the gale
Like the song of a ghost, or a lost angel's wail.
The moan of the death-march, the scream of the fife,
The groan of the drum, like a giant in strife,
Slid into " Sweet Home." Oh exquisitest pain
To the man on the coffin, who hears the refrain,
But can enter home's portals — not ever again!

The doomed is a stranger; and, if he be dear
To a heart in the world, that fond heart is not here.

The multitude comes. The wagon is in sight,
With its grim negro driver, its horses of white,
The man (Christ receive him!) unmoved as a stone
By the terrors before him to which he rides on.
He has done what he could; now all action is gone,
And his undaunted manhood is left him alone.
A small squad of soldiers are there to take part,
Marching on, with arms earthward, beside the old cart.
The skill of a soldier must be a hard art,
With a scant drop of balm for the torturing smart.

They halt. They have reached the unsanctified ground.
The troops in attendance now draw up around
The grim gallows. He stops at the foot of the stair
To strengthen his soul by the magic of prayer.
Oh, how I grew sick as I saw him arise,
Throw a glance on the gallows, then up to the skies!
Then, then, how I wanted the strength of a God
To snatch him from under that chastening rod!
But I was all weakness, the law was all strength,
And he stood in the shadow of darkness at length.
They pinioned his limbs,— how he prayed for God's grace
As they silently drew the white cap o'er his face!

The bolt was withdrawn, and the poor culprit fell
Not dead, — no, not dying, — just hung over hell.

The cotton rope broke, and he fell on the ground,
The hard frozen ground, on the sleet and the snow,
With a shiver of pain, and the mournfulest sound
Which e'er came from man's lips, cold and white as
 the snow.
" Release me, O pitying gazers ! " he cried ;
" Release, O Christ ! who on Calvary died ;
I am innocent still, and my soul is belied."

The multitude shook like a storm-beaten sea,
And they shrieked, " Give him up ! he is free, he is
 free ! "

" He was hanged. He must hang again now *till he
 dies !* "
The word of the statute in silence replies.

The multitude's shrieks sank to murmurous sighs.
Half-stunned and half-conscious they bore him again
To the gallows, to struggles, to death's awful pain ;
They held the bruised culprit erect on the spot,
While they doubled the rope and adjusted the knot ;
They drew the white cap again over his face,
And carefully placed the weak rope in its place ;
And he dropped. Much I hoped he was dangling
 dead ;
But the great knot had slipped to the back of his head,
And he struggled, oh ! fearfully, ere he was dead.

The white cap fell off; and, ah me ! as I write,
I shiver and tremble to think of the sight ;
And I shudder the most that the hearts of God's sons
Are colder and harder than pitiless stones.

If death must be meted, oh! where is the use
Of such merciless torture, demoniac abuse?
We read in high horror of that savage age,
Which stands like a scarecrow on History's page,
When gibbeted victims swung high in the air
Till their flesh all dropped off, and their skeletons
    bare
Clattered in the winds, for the witches and ghosts,
Which thronged round such places in shadowy hosts,
To pick out the teeth, and hunt up locks of hair,
And rattle the bones till they rang on the air
Like gay castanets, and the frightened folks said,
" The witches are revelling over the dead."

O self-righteous Pharisee! empty and vain
Is the hint which you make of superior heart!
How long will the hanged culprit swing in our brain?
How many dark midnights the scared soul will start,
As it dreams of the gallows which snatched up a
    brother,
And choked him from this life into a dim other!
The rope round his neck; and his blackening face;
His eyes, red and bloodshot, forced out of their place;
His horrible writhings; his life-ending pain,—
May I look on such struggles, oh! never again!
He will swing evermore, evermore in my brain.

XXIV.

"CAPTAIN LAGRAVE!" — "Here, sir, is he who
  once was,"
I answered from the very mouth of hell;
While sickeningly I realized the dread cause
  Which made the mournful answer suit me well.
I was a Union prisoner. Do you know
  The living death we drew for rations there?
How life and aspirations sank so low,
  We scarce had energy to feel despair?

Andersonville! When this dread war is over,
  And Justice shall again regain her powers,
Will lovely Nature ever deign to cover
  Your cursed field with emerald grass and flowers?
God can but loathe the place which wrote the record
  Of foul barbarities enacted there;
And, if his work was ever by him abhorred,
  Where should he lavish his contempt but there?

Men went there bearing purpose for endurance,
  And final freedom, and then work again;
But pale Starvation, daily, with a sly lance,
  Stole throbs of life, and left arrows of pain.
Men were not men, but only walking mummies
  Their souls could illy handle for their use.
How could emotions flash themselves from such eyes
  As were all fireless from cruel abuse!

Turned shelterless into a field, with but a blanket,
  And by and by not that, we slept at night
Upon the ground, sometimes with drenching rain
    wet,
  But dreamed of home, and many a dear delight,
And woke to feel the dreadful degradation
  Which hugged us tighter than a boa's coil.
We hunted snails and bugs in our starvation,
  And this vain search made up our daily toil.

To make a nation bend, we bore inflictions
  To which the Inquisition was but play:
We bent not, and we prayed in our afflictions
  The nation would go upright on its way.
Ours was the fate of war: whether imprisoned,
  Or in the field, life was a bitter thing;
A fratricide, becrimsoned and bedizened,
  But sheltered by the plumes of Freedom's wing.

Each heart beat like Regulus'. When endurance
  The life of torture could no longer brave,
Men crossed the "dead line" to the corps of advance,
  Which looks with eagerness across the grave.
We lived, because one cannot die whenever
  Days fall upon the heart like molten lead:
It takes an Atlas' weight of woe to sever
  Body and soul to what mankind call "dead."

We lived, for we were fed a crust of hard-tack,—
  A crumb of putrid flesh, which just sufficed
To keep us breathing, and the Angel Death back,
  Awaiting hourly, at our life surprised.

Sickness came on: among the dead and dying
 I heard their groans, their wants, their cries of
  pain;
And heard our keepers to their plaints replying,
 "Food? water? No! you are detailed for hell
  bane!"

Men licked the very vomit of the dying;
 Gnawed amputated limbs, swollen and red;
And saw their shrivelled skins, all cracked and
  drying,
 Come off in pieces; so much of them dead.
O Freedom! " with your wreath of living eagles,"
 For your sweet sake, your champions bore this all:
Oh, recompense *somebody* for our deep wrongs,
 And mete out honey for our drinking gall!

XXV.

I heard the notes of laughter break
    From a poor ragged fellow,
Whose sad soul seemed at last awake,
    Beneath his face so yellow.

His long stiff hair stood round his face,
    Alive with creeping vermin;
His kith and kin and native place
    His sire could not determine.

He shook himself till you could hear
    Almost his bare bones rattle,
Like musketry which strikes the ear
    In time of a sharp battle.

He held some money o'er his head,
    And cried, " This cash will fill me!
I've long been wanting to be dead;
    I'll *eat* enough to kill me!

" Who wants to join? Come on, my boys,
    I'll buy you a nice dinner;
And, after that, Elysium's joys,
    As sure as I'm a sinner."

Three joined: a lad of seventeen,
    With thin cheeks, pale as ashes;
And two brave men as e'er were seen,
    Who had worn bars and sashes.

They took the food their money bought,
　And thanked Heaven for the weapon
Which it had sent, with sweetness fraught,
　To speed their tortured souls on.

They had a few brief words to send
　To home, with its dear treasures;
Not of their sufferings and end,
　But of the next world's pleasures.

And, while they ate, the Angel Peace
　Folded her wings about them,
And gave their spirits a release,
　Leaving our hell without them.

XXVI.

It was while starving in that loathsome prison,
   A letter (but few reached me) brought a wail
Of sorrow. My sweet sister had arisen
   From our fair home, in a far Western vale,
To a dim country, somewhere in the skies,
Hidden in glory from our longing eyes.
How desolate my grief! in deep distress
I mourned alone, in squalid wretchedness,
To think that she, so innocent and fair,
Must leave her loves, and dwell some otherwhere.

O Death! with crimsoned hands and purpose dark,
Too true, too true, you love a shining mark:
You are a sportsman, with a steady eye,
Beading the bird of the most beauteous dye.
You hear a song, you see a shining head, —
The song is hushed, the singing bird is dead:
The cold wind piping through the autumn skies
Takes the sear leaves, and lets the fresh ones be:
You love the lithest form, the clearest eyes,
The purest souls, — the angels we can see.
What care you who is mad with agony?

I knew at home, beside the azure lake,
   How tears would rain, and smitten hearts would
      break:

I longed to lay one flower on the cold breast,
And let my aching heart break with the rest.

But there, alone, in rags and loneliness,
I drank the bitter cup of my distress,
And almost thought I was unfit to shed
A tear for her, my own, my darling dead.

I knew at home pure taste, at high expense,
Would mourn for her with grand magnificence,
And pyramids of flowers in spotless snow
Be builded, and the saddest music flow;
While gloomiest crape would symbolize the grief
For which there is no balm, no calm relief.

One thing I prayed; that Zylphia's angel-eyes,
Well as I loved her, would not look on me:
I could not bear to think sorrow and sighs
Should fold her spirit in their drapery.

There is a sense of deep relief,
   When those with hearts most pure and true
Pass from this earth of sin and grief,
   Their hopes uncrushed, their sorrows few.
Those who have lived and battled long
   Know of the pangs the soul must feel;
They know how mournful grows life's song,
   And how warm hearts congeal to steel.

Their lids closed over trusting eyes
   Which had not gathered scorns or **jeers**;

Their breasts had heaved to no deep sighs;
   If they had wept, 'twas childish tears.
Their lips grew silent with the lines
   Of hope and sweet assurance wreathed;
Their hands had grasped the wealth that shines
   In words from true affection breathed.

Their memory is a snowy dove
   Perching upon a broken shaft,
An angel with a look of love
   Taking away a glass unquaffed,
And leading, by a willing hand,
   Their spirits by the living streams
Which leap in sunlight through the land
   Of which we catch a glimpse in dreams.

The roses on their tender cheeks
   Stay through the lapse of changing years.
Decay with all his malice wreaks
   His wrath on other heads than theirs.
We live, and see the bits of red
   Fade from our cheeks, our hair turns white:
But sorrows fall not on their dear heads;
   They keep still beautiful and bright.

But oh! I still must deeply mourn
   For the dear sister gone from me;
The snowy hand, the voice of song,
   The precious idol God gave me,
And let me learn to think it mine,
   Then, heeding not my mournful cries,
He moved it to an unknown shrine;
   And what have I but agonies?

XXVII.

MEANWHILE, from the sweet lady of my love
Came not a line to tell my constant heart
I loved her not in vain. I longed to prove
Sometimes that torture's diabolic art
Could wield no power for evil on the soul;
And then again I felt his dread control.
I hoped she would not think of me again;
And, if she thought me dead, would feel no pain,
But love some other, less unfortunate;
While some kind angel showed me through heaven's gate.

But still I felt, if I again were free,
The spark of manhood might yet rally me
To something like my former self; but oh!
My griefs were heavy, and the days moved slow.

XXVIII.

EXCHANGED! I wonder if ever a word
   Sounded as sweet as this.
My heart was glad as a singing bird,
   And crooned to itself its bliss.

Out of the prison-gates we went
   Like a drove of spring-poor cattle,
With hanging heads, and shoulders bent,
   And bones which would almost rattle.

The boat moved off. To her massive wheels
   A few lithe feet were flying,
Dancing, or dancing at, opera-reels,
   While other forms lay a-dying.

We came in sight of the Union fort,
   Where the starry flag waved free;
And there we writhed for the cruel sport
   Of Southern tyranny.

"Let a cheer be raised or a voice be heard
   Cheering that floating rag,
And the man shall go for the slightest word
   Where never shall float that flag!"

We all stood mute, and tears rolled down
   As fast as they could fall:

They could hush our cheers with a threat and
    frown,
But never our hearts at all.

When the shore was gained, and our bondage left
    Aboard with our keepers there,
The blue, blue skies o'er the fort were reft
    With cheers which their ears must bear.

XXIX.

All know, or should, who have an education,
    The greatest evil shrines some dash of good :
That maxim has been preached for consolation
    Since Adam wore Misfortune's cowl and hood,
And needs from me no more elucidation,
    Because it is completely understood.

But I will give myself as an example,
    Begging indulgence. Be it known to you,
I wear a uniform and title ample,
    A trifle cockney, maybe, and both new.
I have the honor to appear a sample
    Of a fresh general in gold and blue.

May Heaven preserve me from the mean delusion
    That with our officers seems to prevail
As soon as they have fairly star or leaf on, —
    That our proud eagle wears a peacock's tail,
And struts about like an inflated turkey,
    Tail-feathers spread, and jetty wings a-trail.

XXX.

I AM going home on furlough :
  Do they think that I am dead?
Do they think that I am sleeping
  Well in a hero's bed,
And can turn not on my pillow
  For all the tears they shed?

I am going home on furlough,—
  Home where the hearts are true ;
But the truest of all is lying
  Under the mourning yew ;
Vacant the splendid prison
  The sweetest of souls looked through!

I am going home on furlough :
  I used to dream of this
When I lay in the Southern prison,
  My poor fate hurled amiss
By a mad, red-handed demon ;
  But I go to a cup of bliss.

I am going home on furlough,
  Clasping hands by the way :
Hurry, O throbbing engine,
  Let us be glad who may !
To-day is shining, to-morrow
  May walk like a nun in gray.

To-night there will be dinner
At the house of Charles Bumare,
And then a brilliant dance ;
When there will be a chance
To bow, if you like, to a British lord,
Stroke his back, and smile at his word,
And see a Southern beauty, refugee,
From a vast estate in Carolina.
A thousand mouths ring out the chime,
" The sweetest lady of the time !"
And I am the lucky sinner
Invited to be there.

XXXI.

THE dinner is over and done;
I danced with the lovely lady, who
Is charming in mind and person too,
And is pledged to the British lord.
She gave me the clear full light of her eyes
From the starriest spot in the midnight skies,
And said, with a trembling touch of surprise,
" Oh, you are so like one in look and bearing,
A friend of mine, who was brave and daring;
Only you are thin and pale, while the other
Was not: you would easily pass for his brother.
He pledged his life to the Union cause,
And died in a horrid prison's jaws.
That is a tale that is told by many;
But my lost friend was bravest of any."
Her cheeks grew pale as a fresh white rose,
And her head bent down like a lily froze,
As her feet moved on in the flying measure,
And her eyes gazed back to her vanished treasure.

She is pledged to the British lord:
  Does she love her English lover?
He speaks to her: every word
  Is a globe of honeyed clover.

She is pledged to the British lord.
  Not improbably she loves him.

I would not doubt her word:
All faultless taste approves him.

Nature made him a splendid work
In point of physical beauty,
And Art had not played the shirk
In doing entirely her duty.

Besides, he has rich broad lands,
And castles rich in story,
Came down through a score of hands,
Proud of their warlike glory.

This was Lord Oakland, come
On a diplomatic mission;
Which failing, he will take home
This splendid acquisition.

Does she love him as she loved one
She speaks of as long since dead?
If she loves as she loved that one,
May the fragrance of poppies be shed
Over his throbbing heart and head!
For he lives, and he is not dead!

But he has not a selfish heart;
He never will break her dream;
For he knows that her bark will start,
Otherwise, down a pleasant stream.
Would he give her milk for cream,
A cloud for a golden gleam?

No! if she has found he is dear
    As the soldier she dreams of as dead,
Then his love shall be laid on a bier,
    And poppies be over it spread;
And it never shall wake up to tread
In her path with its torturing head.

God knows she is dear as my soul;
    And that is the reason I say
My selfishness shall not control
    Me, nor stand in her way.
God strengthen my purpose, I pray,
Lest I stop, and rise up in her way!

On Time! I will see her no more;
    Bear me off o'er the blue bounding lake,
And leave her pure heart to adore,
    While mine shall remember to ache;
But bear for her beautiful sake,
And that not another's may break.

Meanwhile, I shall think of Gazelle
    As tasting all blessings there be;
And I cannot but know it was well
    She married the lord, and not me.
Through massive armorial gates
She will go to the brightest of fates.

Will she weary of pomp and of state?
    Will cares hang upon her young head?
Will her beauty sink with the golden weight,
    And death with her life be fed?
Oh! I hope he will give her a clean warm breast
For her inner life, where her head may rest.

XXXII.

Go by, O weary days!
Go by, O months of bloom!
I am so sad always,
So full of morbid gloom,
I do not like the lights
Which play upon the grass:
The ebon spots of night
Suit best my mood.   Alas!
The flowers I used to love
A great annoyance prove.
The glad birds come to sing
On the warm banks of Spring
No touch of transport bring.
Go by, O weary days!
Go by, O months of bloom!
I am so sad always,
I wish a pitying tomb
Would take me in somewhere, —
Dead me and my despair, —
It is so hard to bear!

XXXIII.

The pealing of the marriage-bell
  Has ceased to shake the air;
Beauty is dead, and music's swell
  Has gone some otherwhere,
While I am moaning here in hell
  To shadowy-eyed Despair.

I saw him in his British pride
  Walk down the twilight aisle,
With grand attendants at his side
  All in superbest style;
And then, ah, Heaven! I cannot tell
  What swept before my sight,
Except I know it was Gazelle
  And twelve maids white as light.

A swell of murmurs met my ear;
  They stood before the altar;
My heart grew still, my eyes grew clear,
  My courage did not falter.
I say, with all my agony,
  My dark self-willed despair,
It was a holy thing to see
  Such perfectness met there.

He was a lord in soul and face,
  Fit for a monarch's throne:

She wore Zenobia's regal grace,
    Her virtues were her own.
Glimmer of silks, and mists of lace,
    And flowers of starry hue,
Were all less fair than the young face
    A seraph soul looked through.
She seemed too deeply fair to wear
    Even Love's flowery chain,
Set here and there with thorns of care
    And hidden shafts of pain.

But trancedly I saw the priest
    Perform the sacred rites;
I thought my mortal life had ceased,
    The dark of all earth's nights
Shut in my soul. I felt as though
    An agonizing soul
Was thrust into a form of snow,
    It warmed not to control.

If she be happy, oh, fly by
    Bright days and sunlit years,
With troops of white doves in your sky,
    And rain not any tears
Upon her head; for, oh, my own
    Bends in the drenching rain!
Leave me to bear this grief alone,
    And love alone in vain.

XXXIV.

I saw her to-night as the charming bride
    She was made a week ago,
The brightest plume on the wing of Pride,
    The gem of the highest glow,
Which flashes for him, and not for me,
    Though its lustre once was mine.
Well, such are the changes on life's wide sea, —
    Clouds after the warm sunshine.

I met her eyes where her thoughts looked out,
    As she and her lord went by;
And I knew she was putting a thought to rout
    That "somebody" did not die.
I hurried on with a careless look,
    And a face as cold as steel;
But my aching heart like a smote harp shook
    With what it must never reveal.

I am chosen to lecture on "Prison Life"
    For the ears of an eager people;
My tongue must picture my own sad life,
    Like the brazen tongue in a steeple.
I shall feel like a loathsome dunghill weed,
    Talking about its former shame;
But Fate cast me, like the tiny seed,
    On filthy soil; I was not to blame.

I am looking, they say, like myself somewhat.
   Nature was ready to build again
On the shattered frame she had better forgot
   In the days of its ruin and pain.

Misfortune has cloaked me in consequence;
   The people are ready to star my name
With bombs of praise, and their love intense
   For heroes centres upon my name
To-morrow night. Alas! I dream
   Of the braver ones who fell
On the weary march, in the prison walls, —
   But who of their fate shall tell?

XXXV.

A SWORD that would honor a victor's hand
   Who had triumphed a thousand times,
The bloodiest Turk in the Turkish lands,
   The Arab of Orient climes,
Was given to me, who had earned it not,
   Last night in a public way.
Was ever a loyal heart forgot,
   That the hand to the heart must sway?

They honored me much. They gave me cheer
   As I talked in my simple way,
Like a child come home to his friends most dear
   After a weary stay.
I felt that the thousand hearts met there
   Beat like a mighty sea:
They bore me up on the wings of prayer,
   As I plead for liberty.

I who had crawled in the very dust,
   Bruised by a tyrant heel,
Told them I knew we could only trust
   Might with her bristling steel.
Brows must pale in the conquering,
   And high hearts cease to beat;
But Right would the compensation bring
   When Wrong lay dead at our feet.

A garnet ring on a handkerchief,
　Wrought with exquisite art,
One threw, bedewed with the drops of grief
　Which rained from a stricken heart;
And oh! before my eyes as I write
　Is a beautiful bouquet
Of rarest blossoms, as fresh and bright
　As the queens of the bloom of May.

But placed with the bright ones, unabashed,
　Is a flower that is dead and dry;
It was long ago that the May-dew flashed
　Like a gem in its azure eye;
And long ago would the winds have torn
　Its petals from off their base,
And none in the world remember or mourn
　O'er the wreck of its beauty and grace.

Who mourns the floweret which died last year,
　Sunk 'neath the cold earth's crust?
Who sheds o'er his ashes the scalding tear
　A hundred years since dust?
O Time! what a wealth of brilliants beam
　Unnoticed upon your brow!
Is there an eye who sees their gleam
　And loves their modest glow?

The flower, embalmed by the touch of care
　From a generation past,
Has come, like an angel in my despair,
　With a gladness which shall not last:
I dream to-night, as I sit alone
　Reading its memoried leaves,

Of a tender face and an earnest tone,
    And the magic of moonlit eves.

And I dream of a lady, proud and grand
    As the eyes of the world can see,
Holding these flowers in her delicate hand
    Before she throws them to me.
No, not to me! — to the general,
    Who is cheered till the crowd is hoarse;
Who went to fight at his country's call, —
    To the general, of course.

But why did she place in the pyramid,
    If she had not a thought of me,
This faded flower, which she has not hid
    By its brilliant rivalry?
Get back, O thought with an adder's sting!
    Get out of my tortured heart!
You drop like a balm from an angel's wing,
    But you end in a torturing smart.

XXXVI.

Fate is fickle, fate is daring,
Ogling, blaming, little caring
Who is white or sable wearing.

Joy from out a life she dashes,
Tears flow off from drooping lashes,
Beauteous forms turn back to ashes.

Shining hopes allure our fancies,
Telling us life's brilliant chances
Fearlessly the soul advances.

Then Fate hurls them in our faces,
Telling us to keep our places,
And not run on bootless chases.

Siren songs she sings, allaying
All the smart; more than repaying
Her unkindness and dismaying.

While we sit meek-faced as Moses,
Certain life is sown with roses,
Stinging bees light on our noses.

Life is but a land of trials,
Sown with cares and self-denials,
Where we drink the " seven vials."

Who relies on Fate's caresses?
If to-day she pets and blesses,
Next we writhe in Sorrow's presses.

Whistle, winds ! cheek, keep your flushes ;
Dauntless heart, endure Grief's crushes ;
Death the wailing one soon hushes.

There, where anguish never rages,
O'er the rolling, rolling ages,
We shall read life's holier pages.

XXXVII.

Excitement is leading the city to-day;
 Regrets are dropping from every mouth;
No heart in the land but recoils in dismay
 At a deed of the warring South.
  Gone is the warmth of a noble heart;
  Cold is a hand Humanity knew;
  Ruined a triumph of Nature's art;
  'Twas a tyrant's hand that slew.

The papers are mourning in sable to-day.
 " A thrilling story!" the newsboys cry;
Arch little faces look up from play,
 And rosy lips shape to a sigh.
  " Where is the lord who was here last week?"
  " What does it read in that column black?"
  Will the heart of the lovely lady break
   That he never can come back? ·

" Was it a duel?" the small boys ask;
 " Who dared to strike him upon the mouth?"
Preaching Right is a perilous task
 In the land we call the South!
  Lord Oakland held negro suffrage
   Just; in an amiable debate
  His colleague flew in an insolent rage,
   And struck the lord in his hate.

He thrust him off with a practised arm
  Which laid the Southerner low ;
He felt not harmed, and he did no harm, —
  The one with a calm, high brow.
    Not so the one who was weak in soul ;
      He waved in anger his cold blue steel,
    And cried, "O God, thou mayst damn my soul,
      But his proud blood must congeal ! "

He sprang like a tiger quick and sly ;
  His steel leaped into the noble breast.
Lord Oakland fell on the floor to die ;
  The Southerner killed his guest !
    That is the way that the great man died,
      Only for speaking his honest mind ;
    O chivalry of the Southern pride !
      Are you maniac or blind ?

XXXVIII.

Is the sun of heaven painting
    Rainbows on a shower of tears?
Is a giant sorrow fainting,
    Plodding through the weary years?
Like dim dreams I had in childhood,
    Vanished years come back to me,
Whispering of lake and wildwood
    In a land across the sea.

Gorgeously the morn is breaking
    Down into a cup-like vale,
Where the ancient trees are shaking
    Glad hands with an English gale.
Hawthorn hedges white with blossoms,
    Flinging fragrance faint and rare,
Heave the chaste snow of their bosoms
    To the sun and luscious air.

Caring nothing for the gladness
    Nature feels, the manor stands
Like a grand colossal sadness,
    Petted by the million hands
Of the ivy, dark and solemn,
    Rooted in the choicest mould,
Clinging upon arch and column
    With a never-loosing hold.

Now the sunlight gilds the pictures
  Looking from their massive frames;
Yonder hangs one with gold fixtures,
  Which my holiest reverence claims.
It was done across the ocean
  By a famous master's hand;
It commands the soul's devotion
  By its calm power, high and grand.

'Tis the late young lord of Oakland,
  And his Southern bride, Gazelle,
Painted for an absence offering
  Just before his lordship fell.
Stricken down, when life was flushing,
  By a tyrant's mad caprice,
Though heaven's brightest bliss stooped blushing,
  His was not a sweet release.

Oh the heart with bleeding gushes,
  Moaning for him day by day!
Oh the fresh cheeks turned to ashes,
  Eyes where midnight shadows lay!
She is mine now. Flowers are growing
  On the pure heart's shattered shrine;
But I sadden sometimes, knowing
  How it is that she is mine.
Then she puts a snowy finger
  On the scant red of my lips,
Asking why "the shadows linger
  Darkling after the eclipse."

Life is steeped at last in sweetness
   Perfect as my early dream ;
Silken sails bear on with fleetness
   Our bright shallops down Time's stream.
Here among these scenes we linger,
   For *his* holy memory's sake ;
But Love stretches a white finger
   Toward a home beside a lake.

WORSHIP.

The first warm dews of spring-time
  Shine on the grass to-night;
The air is moist and luscious,
  And to breathe it is delight.
My heart is full of worship
  For the beautiful and true;
So come and sit beside me, love,
  And let me worship you.
    A hand for a hand,
    A smile for a kiss;
    Heart-thrill for heart-thrill,
    And bliss for bliss.

My heart is full of worship;
  And the pearly moon I view,
Or the stars, or trees, would own it
  If I ne'er had worshipped you.
But all things which I have dreamed of,
  Or the fair earth shown to me,
Are less beautiful and holy
  Than thy great soul's destiny.
    A hand for a hand,
    A smile for a kiss;
    Heart-thrill for heart-thrill,
    And bliss for bliss.

Sit where the mellow sunbeams
  Will light your pensive brow;
I want to touch it now and then,
  And to its wisdom bow.
Oh! let me learn the lessons
  Which lie in your clear eyes;
You learned them from the sainted souls
  Who reach you from the skies.
    A hand for a hand,
      A smile for a kiss;
    Heart-thrill for heart-thrill,
      And bliss for bliss.

My heart is formed for worship,
  Like the birds for minstrelsy,
And thy perfectness has won it
  From its vain idolatry
Of poems, pictures, statues —
  Beauteous but pulseless clay —
That which could never love me
  Had I worshipped life away.
    A hand for a hand,
      A smile for a kiss,
    Heart-thrill for heart-thrill,
      And bliss for bliss.

"WE WRITE BLESSINGS IN SAND, EVILS IN MARBLE."

I saw a young girl with an innocent brow,
And eyes to which beautiful Juno would bow,
And cheeks that were glowing with roses and health,
Bow her head on her hand, and sigh, " If I had wealth !
My efforts for happiness all seem in vain,
My beauty is nothing, my dress is so plain ;
Compared with a *lady*, I merit disdain ;
And I own it were stoical not to complain.
My parents are old-fashioned people, although
They are upright and loving and noble, I know,
But the last in the country to make any show.
I am quite out of place in this glittering world,
And the darts of misfortune upon me are hurled."

It is strange, it is strange, that our minds are so planned,
We write evils on marble, and blessings on sand !

I looked on a poet with that on his face
Which nought but Divinity's finger can trace ;
A heart in his bosom which happiness caught
From the great soul of Nature, and throbbed into thought ;

Thought burst into music, and music took wings.
And whispered the listener of rapturous things;
Dim eyes were turned skyward, wan faces grew bright,
And the sinner grew heart-sick, and searched for the Right.
Oh! nothing can rob him of pleasure, I said,
With his great, loving heart, and his great, thinking head;
But a beautiful lady rejected his hand,
And married his rival, with houses and land.
She chose to wear diamonds in tangible shape:
So the poet sold his, and bought jet and black crape;
Bankrupted his brain, and, in face of his God,
He cursed his existence, and frowned on the rod.

It is strange, it is strange, that the mind is so planned,
We write evils in marble, and blessings in sand!

I saw a fond husband. The joy of his life
Was a bright, laughing boy, and a true-hearted wife.
He builded a home filled with beautiful things,
As costly and grand as the castles of kings.
Chill airs never blew on the idols he loved,
And the world bowed before him wherever he moved.
He laughed at the luck which had filled to the brim
His goblet of gold, while his brothers had tin,
And scantily filled. But reverses came on;
And, ere he scarce knew it, his riches were gone.
A strange freak of fortune, which favored mankind,
Dispersed them, like thistle-downs thrown to the wind.
Love still wore its evergreens, — they are the same
In palace or cottage; want, even in name,

Was a stranger ; but nothing of joy could he borrow :
Who ate cream yesterday must have cream for to-
    morrow.
His ill-gotten splendors he could not forget ;
And he died — died a victim to foolish regret.

It is strange, it is strange, that the mind is so planned,
We write evils on marble, and blessings in sand !

I saw an old man, who was nearing the tomb ;
He knew that it led into glory through gloom :
His life had been long, his adversities few ;
His nights broke in sunshine, his clouds into blue ;
His children were dutiful, talented, true ;
His wife had as much as Penelope's truth,
And she loved him in age as she loved him in youth.
He, too, was forgetful. He shook his white head,
" This world is all emptiness," gravely he said ;
" Our hopes are delusive, our joys only bawbles ;
We have one enjoyment to legions of troubles ! "

It is strange, it is strange, that the mind is so planned,
We write evils on marble, and blessings in sand !

THE HERO'S BURIAL.

Lead out the pageant for the brave
You bear to fill a soldier's grave;
Not with a step so sad and slow
As suits an unillumined woe.
He was a hero: he had thought
How bravery is often bought;
He knew he might be lying here
Just as he is; and yet no fear
Guested a moment in his breast.
He was a hero: let him rest.

Well has he done a tragic part,
And bravely met the venomed dart,
With no repining at the smart.
Before he went, he plucked his heart
From his young breast; that was a pain
Scarce less than that of being slain.
He loved his wife, he loved his child;
He knew, although he said, and smiled,
"I shall come back," the time and way
Were left for changeful Fates to say.
He knew it might be as it is, —
No pulse, motion, or language his
To greet the many thronging here
To see him on his bier.

He knew it would be sad to lie,
The cause of many a broken sigh,
And breaking heart, and streaming eye;
And yet he weighed the matter well,
And took the Right with what befell:
He chose it: we must not rebel.
But oh! — perhaps it is a sin —
I would to God this had not been! —
That black spot on his broad, white brow
Which laid him where we see him now.
How strange it is such little things
Can send souls off to heaven on wings!
One could not tell a reason why
He on a dead man's bier should lie,
But for that spot the bullet made,
So slight, but deadly as the blade.

His life is gone, but not in vain;
Breathe joy into the sad refrain.
A mighty wrong is dying out;
Dumb tongues have learned that they can shout;
Long buried souls are cropping out;
He died to bring this change about!

Fond parents, think it was for this
   You reared him all these hopeful years;
Not that your high words worked amiss,
   And honor brought you these hot tears.
Better to die in such a work,
   Accomplishing gigantic uses,
Than live eternities a shirk,
   Bearing through time one's own abuses.

'Tis hard to dote for twenty years
  On talents cultured 'neath your eye
For actions grand. But dry your tears;
  A noble soul can never die.
Your every word of wisdom given
Will be remembered still in heaven;
Your sanctifying love will be
A sweet through all eternity.

LITTLE ZOE.

" MY WIFE."

Yes, she's a trump, my pretty Zoe,
   My bright Italian bride;
I must look handsomer myself
   When she is by my side.
It flies and warms from lip to lip
   In New York bon-ton life,
The praise of this exported flower,
   And that she is — my wife.

A diamond of the purest rate —
   Pardon me this — am I;
An alpha in the dollar scale,
   My father ranked as high.
Position, homage, beauty, gold,
   Are shining round my life;
Ah, very blest is little Zoe,
   Because she is — my wife.

A bandeau for her shining head
   Gleaming with diamond stars,
And Venus for her Parian breast
   Caged by four golden bars;

Fabrics as costly as a queen's
  Shall drape her form of grace;
French rose-buds, and a cloud of lace,
  Nestle about her face.

A splendid home shall be her own;
  The carpeting shall fill
The high arch of her Arab foot,
  And all things please her will.
She must be fairest of the fair,
  Witty, and gay, and blithe,
Dance like a fairy, play and sing,
  Because she is — my wife.

A tear! a tear! and when she dies,
  Thank fate! I have the gold
To buy a splendid monument,
  To tell, as years grow old,
How consequential was my wife:
  It is no idle thing
For Zoe to be the richest plume
  Upon a gorgeous wing.

CHANGELESS.

I was fever-parched and weary,
　With a loveless, drooping head,
Mourning for its stolen treasures;
　Can you love me now? I said.
Tenderly he twined my fingers,
　Telling me how much he missed me;
Home was desolate without me;
　And he smoothed my hair, and kissed me.

Dry, parched lips, ye had no sweetness
　He could garner, well I know;
But from off his lips of sunset
　To my hollow cheek of snow
Stole a glow which staid and deepened
　Every time he bent and kissed me,
Softly breathing the assurance
　That in sickness he had missed me.

Each blue veinlet on my forehead
　Soothingly his finger traced,
One by one each tangled ringlet
　Coiled around his finger graced.
All my soul went out in blessing
　For the love which will not falter,
Burning through Time's myriad changes
　On the soul's decayless altar.

THE DRAGOON'S RETREAT.

Out of the way of the fighters, here to the shady wood,
Bloody, and faint, and aching, I have crawled as best
    I could.
I hate this way of retreating, now while my fiery heart
Thumps to be helping my comrades, till my wounds
    gape wide apart
To let the great streams of blood out, — I hate to see
    it flow;
It is free, and strong, and loyal, and should not be
    wasted so.

It hurts me to fly from battle, to join in this still re-
    treat;
With the rest of the shot and dying, to join the spirit
    retreat
Into the land of Silence, into the land of Peace!
I'd rather stay in the battle till all the soldiers cease;
But I'm going farther off than the wildwood here;
I can hardly raise my canteen, I can scarcely see or
    hear.

O home! O love! lost heaven! I know how the sullen
    word
"Shot!" will moan round the fireside, and a deep
    regret be stirred

That they ever gave their Percy to fight for the trampled Right!
I wish their dear eyes could see me, here in the waning light;
Each tender grass-leaf trying to pillow my dizzy head:
This mound here is just as easy as the downiest dying bed.

I am tired — this seems like resting — four days in a raging fight,
For a boy like me, a novice; but I see I shall sleep to-night
So deep, that the cannon's thunder, nor a shout of victory,
Could wake my body to shouting; but then 'twill not be me.
Dumb tongue, still heart, I've a spirit which burns like the northern star,
And will then, even then, be pulsing for Right and the Union war!

Retreating! how faint comes the tumult which croaks o'er the gory field!
The forms of yon blue-mailed warriors are only half revealed;
But, oh! a rout! they are coming! well, it is spared from me
To ride with the hunted soldiers in the crazy cavalry:
I'm passed to another army, where men like Ellsworth stand,
And we all shall serve our country yet, in the spirit-land.

THE FRIEND I HAD.

On the damp air the funeral knell
    Sounds o'er the hills in measured tone.
Oh! cease to toll, thou solemn bell;
    Let me forget my friend is gone.
Four suns ago, and she was here
    Beside me in this quiet room,
Irradiating her good cheer:
    Now she is shrouded for the tomb!
Oh! thus it is Life's tempest-shocks
Bruise us upon the hidden rocks.

She left me, kissing me good-by,
    And promising to come again;
And yet — I cannot tell you why,
    My very heart cried out in pain
To see the carriage wheel away.
    I thought 'twas but a silly whim,
And hoped to see her in a day —
    It was a warning, shadowed, dim.
Oh, well! she was a precious saint!
A mortal with no mortal taint!

Last morn upon my horse I sprang,
    And galloped to her father's door
While yet the early robins sang,
    To chat an hour, as oft before.

I met her brother at the gate,
  As pale as stone: he turned away.
" Is that your gallantry of late ?"
  I said.   " How is my friend to-day?"
He knit his brows, he dropped his head,
And hoarsely stammered, " She is dead!"
. . . .
Dear girl! her earthly life was brief,
  But balmed by love's most precious dew:
Now she has passed beyond all grief,
  Where life is roseate and new.
Cry out, my heart, cry out in pain!
  Nurse if you will your selfish grief;
Your loss is her uncounted gain;
  But sorrow till you find relief.
I know to-night her head is prest
Upon her angel mother's breast.

SADNESS.

Well, Sadness, thou and I have come
    To be boon friends at last;
The shadows in thy swimming eyes
    Upon my own are cast;
The lines about my silent mouth
    Are fashioning like thine:
I never thought that I should come
    To bow before thy shrine.

You, Sadness, are a little child,
    Mystic and sweet and calm;
And those may think, who know you not,
    You wear a wreath of balm.
You play to-day in innocence,
    With a bright, feathered arrow,
Which in your hands will pierce men's hearts,
    When you grow into sorrow.

Oh! shall I be your chosen friend
    When you grow into sorrow?
And will it be my throbbing breast
    Which meets the stinging arrow?
Ah yes! I read the prophecy:
    You cling so fondly to me,
I know that you will stay with me;
    Oh, do no bad thing through me!

HALLY.

With the engine I am flying
    Through the quiet Mohawk Valley,
O'er the ground, and through the sunshine,
    Where in youth I used to dally
With gay Time and rosy maidens;
    And a thought comes up of Hally.

Hally, tall and very graceful,
    Hally with her bright black eyes,
Hally with her voice of music,
    Thrilling whispers, dainty sighs, —
Oh, her lips of sun-dyed coral
    Yielded many sweet replies!

I was then a lad of twenty;
    Hally was but seventeen:
I was dashing, gay, and handsome;
    Hally wore a lowly mien.
If conceit were good at wooing,
    I'd enough to win a queen.

There I see a group of willows,
    An old trysting-place of ours,
Where one moonrise hour I told her
    She had best go gathering flowers

Through the blossoming land of beaux-hearts,
    And forget the passing hours.

That bright eve we walked together
    For an hour the self-same track :
When we reached the vine-clasped cottage,
    She went in, and I turned back.
Since that day we both have travelled
    Life's strange ways in diverse track.

Shall I murmur? I ordained it ;
    But my heart would know less pain
Could I hope that in the coming
    Time we e'er could walk again
Onward in the same old pathway ;
    But I know the wish is vain.

Finding no true heart to love me,
    I have given gold my vow ;
Thoughtful Hally stands above me,
    Wisdom's baptism on her brow.
We must walk apart forever ;
    Hally could not love me now.

ANNA SHADER.

WHERE, oh, where, is Anna Shader,
With a heart like summer song-birds,
Gushing out its rills of music,
And a form to match in beauty
Her pure soul which daily won us?
She had hair like braids of satin
Glowing o'er her dovelike forehead;
She had eyes like fairy blue-bells,
With a diamond dropped within them;
She had cheeks that mocked the wild-rose;
And like honeysuckle blossoms
Freshened with night dews her lips were.

Where is gentle Anna Shader?
Night winds moaning through yon hemlocks,
Whispering round the marble head-stones
Read upon one leant and lowly,
Tell of blighted Anna Shader;
Whisper how she paled and vanished
Like a star into the heavens.
Whisper — oh, forget to whisper
That her unwise loving slew her;
For I bruised the snowy lily,
Tore the gauzy wings in pieces,
Covered them with dust and ruin.

GOOD-BY.

Good-by, good-by, I speak it now,
    Before you pass from hearing;
The time may come when I and thou
    Shall miss things most endearing.
I trust no sorrow on thy head
    May fall; and as I love thee,
I trust o'er roses thou mayst tread
    Up to the heaven above thee.

Oh, turn not from thy happiness
    To think of fond eyes weeping!
For, through my bitterest distress,
    A final peace is creeping.
I care not if it blanch my face,
    And steal its bits of carmine;
I care not now, for its slight grace
    Is thrust from all that's divine.

Pass on thy way, so dazzling bright;
    I know thou wilt forget me.
I fly into a rainy night,
    And no one will regret me.
Good-by! God grant thou mayst not think
    My sable sin was loving,
Nor fathom why my heart should shrink
    From the cold world's reproving!

www.ingramcontent.com/pod-product-compliance
Lightning Source LLC
Chambersburg PA
CBHW030819190426
43197CB00036B/605